Landmarks of world literature

Fyodor Dostoyevsky

THE BROTHERS KARAMAZOV

Landmarks of world literature

General Editor: J. P. Stern

Dickens: *Bleak House* – Graham Storey
Homer: *The Iliad* – Michael Silk
Dante: *The Divine Comedy* – Robin Kirkpatrick
Rousseau: *Confessions* – Peter France
Goethe: *The Sorrows of Young Werther* – Martin Swales
Constant: *Adolphe* – Dennis Wood
Balzac: *Old Goriot* – David Bellos
Mann: *Buddenbrooks* – Hugh Ridley
Homer: *The Odyssey* – Jasper Griffin
Tolstoy: *Anna Karenina* – Anthony Thorlby
Conrad: *Nostromo* – Ian Watt
Camus: *The Stranger* – Patrick McCarthy
Murasaki Shikibu: *The Tale of Genji* – Richard Bowring
Sterne: *Tristram Shandy* – Wolfgang Iser
Shakespeare: *Hamlet* – Paul A. Cantor
Stendhal: *The Red and the Black* – Stirling Haig
Brontë: *Wuthering Heights* – U. C. Knoepflmacher
Pasternak: *Doctor Zhivago* – Angela Livingstone
Proust: *Swann's Way* – Sheila Stern
Pound: *The Cantos* – George Kearns
Beckett: *Waiting for Godot* – Lawrence Graver
Chaucer: *The Canterbury Tales* – Winthrop Wetherbee
Virgil: *The Aeneid* – K. W. Gransden
García Márquez: *One Hundred Years of Solitude*
  – Michael Wood
Cervantes: *Don Quixote* – A. J. Close
Céline: *Journey to the End of the Night* – John Sturrock
Boccaccio: *Decameron* – David Wallace
Wordsworth: *The Prelude* – Stephen Gill
Eliot: *Middlemarch* – Karen Chase
Hardy: *Tess of the d'Urbervilles* – Dale Kramer
The Bible – Stephen Prickett and Robert Barnes
Flaubert: *Madame Bovary* – Stephen Heath
Baudelaire: *Les Fleurs du Mal* – F. W. Leakey
Zola: *L'Assommoir* – David Baguley
Boswell: *The Life of Johnson* – Greg Clingham
Pushkin: *Eugene Onegin* – A. D. P. Briggs
Dostoyevsky: *The Brothers Karamazov* – W. J. Leatherbarrow
Galdós: *Fortunata and Jacinta* – Harriet S. Turner
Aeschylus: *The Oresteia* – Simon Goldhill
Byron: *Don Juan* – Anne Barton
Lawrence: *Sons and Lovers* – M. H. Black

FYODOR DOSTOYEVSKY:

The Brothers Karamazov

W. J. LEATHERBARROW

*Senior Lecturer, Department of Russian
and Slavonic Studies,
University of Sheffield*

CAMBRIDGE
UNIVERSITY PRESS

Published by the Press Syndicate of the University of Cambridge
The Pitt Building, Trumpington Street, Cambridge CB2 1RP
40 West 20th Street, New York NY 10011-4211, USA
10 Stamford Road, Oakleigh, Victoria 3166, Australia

First published 1992

Printed in Great Britain at the University Press, Cambridge

A catalogue record for this book is available from the British Library

Library of Congress cataloguing in publication data

Leatherbarrow, William J.
Fyodor Dostoyevsky – The brothers Karamazov/W. J. Leatherbarrow.
    p.   cm. – (Landmarks of world literature)
Includes bibliographical references.
ISBN 0 521 38424 9 (hardback). – ISBN 0 521 38601 2 (paperback)
1. Dostoyevsky, Fyodor, 1821–1881. Brat′ia Karamazovy.
I. Title. II. Series.
PG3325.B73L4 1992
891.73′3 – dc20   91-43123 CIP

ISBN 0 521 38424 9 hardback
ISBN 0 521 38601 2 paperback

WG

For Vivien

Contents

Note on the text   *page* ix
Chronology   x

Introduction   1

1   *The background to the novel*   4

2   *The novel*   21

     The family   21
     The fragmented hero   30
     The quest for harmony   42
     Pro and contra   59
     'A realist in a higher sense'   81

3   *The critical reception*   98

Guide to further reading   112

Note on the text

The Brothers Karamazov consists of twelve books and an epilogue, each of which is subdivided into chapters. References to passages quoted or mentioned are to book and chapter rather than to a particular edition. All translations from the novel are my own. No footnotes are given, but reference is made, where essential, to critical studies listed in the guide to further reading. This in turn does not pretend to bibliographical completeness: it is confined to a list of titles cited or consulted in the preparation of this volume and to works of particular value for the student or general reader. Where extracts from Dostoyevsky's other works, articles or letters are given, reference is made by volume and page number (e.g. XV, 200) to the thirty-volume *Nauka* edition of his complete works, *Polnoye sobraniye sochineniy v tridtsati tomakh*. Where the Nauka publishers have split a volume in two, separately bound parts, an additional number appears after the volume number (e.g. XXX/1). Publication of this fine edition commenced in 1972 and it now approaches completion.

Finally, I should like to express my gratitude to Twayne Publishers, a division of G.K. Hall & Co., Boston, Mass., USA, for permission to use material originally published in chapter seven of my study, *Fedor Dostoevsky* (1981).

Chronology

	Dostoyevsky's life and works	Major literary and historical events
1821	Born in Moscow at the Mariinsky hospital for the poor, where his father worked as a doctor.	
1823–31		Pushkin: *Eugene Onegin*.
1825		Decembrist Revolt and accession of Nicholas I.
1828		Birth of Tolstoy.
1830		Stendhal: *Le Rouge et le Noir*.
1831	Sees production of Schiller's *The Robbers* which affects him deeply.	
1833–7	At school in Moscow.	
1834		Pushkin: *The Queen of Spades*.
1835		Balzac: *Le Père Goriot*.
1836		Gogol: *The Government Inspector*.
1837	Death of mother. Enters St Petersburg Academy of Military Engineering.	Death of Pushkin. Dickens: *Pickwick Papers*.
1839	Death of father in mysterious circumstances.	Stendhal: *The Charterhouse of Parma*.
1840		Lermontov: *A Hero of Our Time*.
1841	Attempts to write plays.	Death of Lermontov.
1842		Gogol: *Dead Souls* and 'The Overcoat'.
1843	Graduates from Military Academy.	

1844	Resigns commission in order to devote himself to literature. First published work: a translation of Balzac's *Eugénie Grandet*.	
1845	Finishes *Poor Folk*. Meets Belinsky.	
1846	*Poor Folk* published to widespread acclaim. A more subdued reception given to *The Double*. Epilepsy diagnosed.	
1847	'The Landlady'. Starts to attend meetings of the Petrashevsky circle.	Emigration of Herzen.
1848	'A Faint Heart' and 'White Nights'.	Revolutions in Europe. Death of Belinsky. Thackeray: *Vanity Fair*.
1849	*Netochka Nezvanova*. Becomes involved with more radical section of the Petrashevsky circle. April 23: arrested and imprisoned in the Peter and Paul Fortress, where he writes *A Little Hero*. November: Commission of Inquiry reports and sentences Dostoyevsky to death. December: mock execution. Death sentence commuted to Siberian hard labour and exile.	Russia invades Hungary.
1850	Arrives at Omsk prison settlement.	Dickens: *David Copperfield*.
1851		World Exhibition at Crystal Palace, London.
1852		Death of Gogol. Tolstoy: *Childhood*. Turgenev: *A Sportsman's Sketches*.
1853–6		Crimean War.
1854	Hard labour ends. Posted to Semipalatinsk as a common soldier.	

1855		Chernyshevsky joins *The Contemporary*. Death of Nicholas I and accession of Alexander II amidst hopes of social and political reform.
1856		Turgenev: *Rudin*.
1857	Marries Maria Dmitryevna Isayeva.	Flaubert: *Madame Bovary*. Baudelaire: *Les Fleurs du Mal*.
1859	*The Village of Stepanchikovo* and 'Uncle's Dream'. December: returns to St Petersburg.	Turgenev: *A Nest of Gentlefolk*. Goncharov: *Oblomov*. Tolstoy: *Family Happiness*. Darwin: *The Origin of Species*.
1860	Starts publication of *The House of the Dead*.	Turgenev: *On the Eve*. Birth of Chekhov. George Eliot: *The Mill on the Floss*.
1861	Starts publication of moderate periodical *Time*. *The Insulted and Injured*.	Emancipation of the serfs. Formation of revolutionary organization *Land and Liberty*.
1862	Travels in Europe. Affair with Polina Suslova.	Turgenev: *Fathers and Sons*. Tense revolutionary mood in St Petersburg. *The Contemporary* suspended and Chernyshevsky arrested. Hugo: *Les Misérables*.
1863	*Winter Notes on Summer Impressions*. Closure of *Time*. Further travels in Europe with Suslova.	Polish uprising. Tolstoy: *The Cossacks*. Chernyshevsky: *What is to be Done?*
1864	Launches *The Epoch*. *Notes from Underground*. Deaths of wife and brother Mikhail.	The First International. Student unrest in Kazan. Legal reforms in Russia, including introduction of trial by jury. Dickens: *Our Mutual Friend*.
1865	Financial collapse of *The Epoch*. Severe financial difficulties. Starts work on *Crime and Punishment*.	
1865–9		Tolstoy: *War and Peace*.
1866	Publishes *Crime and Punishment*. Writes *The Gambler* in twenty-six days with help of stenographer Anna Grigoryevna Snitkina.	Attempted assassination of Alexander II by Dmitry Karakozov.

1867	Marries Anna Grigoryevna. Flees abroad to escape creditors. Meets Turgenev in Baden. Visits Dresden and Geneva.	Turgenev: *Smoke*.
1868	Still abroad. Death of infant daughter. *The Idiot*.	
1869	Returns to Dresden and plans 'The Life of a Great Sinner'.	Murder of student Ivanov in Moscow by Nechayev's political circle.
1870	*The Eternal Husband*.	Defeat of France in Franco-Prussian War. Death of Herzen. Birth of V.I. Ulyanov (Lenin).
1871	Returns to St Petersburg.	Defeat of Paris Commune.
1871–2	*The Devils*.	
1872	Becomes editor of *The Citizen*.	Trial of Nechayev. Leskov: *Cathedral Folk*. Marx's *Das Kapital* published in Russia.
1873	Begins *The Diary of a Writer*.	Attempts by thousands of Russian students to provoke revolutionary unrest amongst peasantry.
1874	Resigns from *The Citizen*. Visits Bad Ems for treatment for emphysema.	Political strikes in Odessa.
1875	*A Raw Youth*.	Tolstoy: *Anna Karenina*.
1975–8		Russia declares war on Turkey. Turgenev: *Virgin Soil*.
1977		Death of Nekrasov. Arrest and trial of Vera Zasulich.
1978	Death of son Alexey. Visit to Optina Monastery with Solovyov.	
1879–80	*The Brothers Karamazov* (completed November 1880).	Tolstoy's religious crisis, during which he writes *A Confession*.
1880	Delivers the Pushkin Speech.	
1880–1	Final issues of *The Diary of a Writer*.	

1881	January 28: dies in St Petersburg. February 1: funeral in Alexander Nevsky Monastery attended by over thirty thousand people.	Assassination of Alexander II.
1883		Death of Turgenev. Nietzsche: *Thus Spake Zarathustra*.
1889		Death of Chernyshevsky.
1904		Death of Chekhov.
1910		Death of Tolstoy.
1912		Constance Garnett's English translation of *The Brothers Karamazov*.

Introduction

The Brothers Karamazov has long had the reputation of being an 'important book', a 'landmark of world literature'. This is, as the present study hopes to show, a richly deserved reputation, but it is also in some senses an unfortunate one. More often than not, the novel has been approached by the new reader as a hostile peak to be scaled by the ambitious intelligence, or as a form of particularly strenuous intellectual weight-training to be endured with gritted teeth in the hope of enhanced mental muscularity and fitness. This is regrettable, for *The Brothers Karamazov* turns out to be an enjoyable and accessible novel which fully displays Dostoyevsky's mastery as a storyteller, as well as his significance as a thinker.

The main plot is remarkably simple, although it supports a wide range of secondary developments. As in many of Dostoyevsky's earlier works, murder and money dominate the action. Fyodor Pavlovich Karamazov, a corrupt and lascivious provincial landowner, is the father of three legitimate sons: Dmitry, a retired army officer; Ivan, a brilliant intellectual; and Alyosha, a novice monk under the tutelage of the local monastic elder, Father Zosima. Dmitry is the child of Fyodor Pavlovich's first marriage, Ivan and Alyosha the sons of his second. Fyodor is also the suspected father of an illegitimate son, Smerdyakov, the result of a liaison with a local idiot girl, Liza Smerdyashchaya. Smerdyakov now works as a servant in the Karamazov household.

When Fyodor Pavlovich is found murdered, suspicion falls on Dmitry, although we later learn that the crime was committed by Smerdyakov. Dmitry's violent nature and his conviction that he has been cheated out of his inheritance have already led to furious scenes between him and his father. What is more, father and son are locked in dangerous sexual rivalry

1

over a local seductress, Grushenka, whose charms have already enticed Dmitry away from his betrothed, Katerina. All this points to Dmitry's guilt, and he is arrested. At his trial things go badly for him and he is sentenced to Siberia. Grushenka, now reformed, decides to accompany him and Katerina remains to look after Ivan, whose mental breakdown follows recognition of Smerdyakov's guilt and the role played in his father's murder by his own conversations with the lackey. But nothing can be proved. Dmitry goes to serve his sentence, Smerdyakov commits suicide, Ivan succumbs to his illness, and the novel ends with Alyosha leaving the monastery and following Zosima's advice to go out into the world.

If the novel's plot is simple, its thematic preoccupations and artistic innovations are startlingly ambitious. It addresses such major themes as atheism and belief, the nature of man, socialism and individualism, freedom and justice, and the state of European civilisation in an artistic form that both draws on existing novelistic tradition and prepares the way for many of the directions taken by the genre in the twentieth century. Essentially, it is a novel concerned with confrontations between order and disorder, justice and injustice, harmony and chaos, unity and fragmentation, and it evolves a distinctive artistic form and apt narrative strategies to convey its thematic concerns. It explores these confrontations in a variety of settings, including the psychological, the familial, the social, the moral and the metaphysical. In all these manifestations it seeks to show man the way forward from what Dostoyevsky saw as the underlying disorder of his age into a new state of moral and spiritual certainty rooted in the author's own convictions as an Orthodox Christian. In this respect *The Brothers Karamazov* is an overtly didactic work, a great achievement of Christian literature, although it manages to avoid the dogmatic and the stridently evangelical. It is not to be read simply as a religious tract: it is, in the end, the result of a lifetime's reflection on the most burning issues of the age by a novelist celebrated even in his own time for his penetrating insights, prophetic vision and revolutionary approach to the art of fiction.

I have in this study sought to avoid writing an all-embracing introductory prospectus to the novel. To try to cover all that it has to offer in a work of this kind would be to risk skimping on everything. In any case such a task has been admirably accomplished by the American scholar, Victor Terras (*A Karamazov Companion*). Instead, I have attempted a unified analysis centred upon the novel's preoccupation with justice, order and disorder, for it is in the revolutionary artistic treatment of these themes that its real significance as a literary landmark lies.

Chapter 1

The background to the novel

Well, the novel is finished! I have worked on it for three years, and have been publishing it [in instalments] for two — a significant moment for me ... With your permission I won't take my leave of you. After all, I intend to live and write for another twenty years.

(XXX/1, 227)

The Dostoyevsky who in November 1880, just two months before his death, so announced the completion of *The Brothers Karamazov* to N. A. Lyubimov, the associate editor of *Russkii vestnik* (The Russian Herald), was far removed from the young man who in the 1840s had gained fame as the author of tales of psychological analysis and had then suffered arrest, mock execution and Siberian exile for participation in an illegal political group. This group, the Petrashevsky circle, had been broken up by the police in April 1849 and its members charged with 'revolutionary' plotting and subversive acts against the tsarist regime. Dostoyevsky and the other ringleaders were subjected to a grim reminder of monarchical power: a death sentence commuted only seconds before its execution to, in Dostoyevsky's case, four years of imprisonment with hard labour followed by a further four years of exile.

Dostoyevsky had associated with the most radical wing of the Petrashevsky circle, but his subsequent experience of the criminal mind during his years of imprisonment and hard labour had stripped him of his earlier political idealism and convinced him of the powerlessness of reason — and the moral and political programmes it supports — to resurrect the depraved human soul and usher in a new era of justice and social harmony. He retained until the end of his life a powerful vision of a Golden Age of primeval innocence, when men would live like brothers in a harmonious state of love and mutual regard, but he had lost forever the belief that this ideal might be achieved by political means. His experiences of the effects of capitalism and bourgeois greed during his first European tour in 1861 had further convinced him that 'we do not have a nature capable of brotherhood' (V, 81), and in his polemical account of his European travels, *Winter Notes on Summer Impressions* (1863), he dismissed pure reason and the solutions it purported to offer as 'that unfounded fiction of the eighteenth century' (V, 78).

The period of Siberian exile thus marked Dostoyevsky's retreat from rational humanism and political idealism. Instead, he resumed his literary career at the end of the 1850s as a writer with a religious mission, dedicated to the belief that salvation could be achieved only with the complete moral transformation of human nature through love, suffering and the experience of Christ. Indeed, he confessed that he drew strength during the dark years of his imprisonment and degradation largely from his copy of the New Testament, which, battered and much-annotated, still survives in the Dostoyevsky archives. His journalistic activities and literary works of the 1860s and 1870s clearly reveal his essentially religious vision. As the editor of the periodicals *Vremya* (Time) and *Epokha* (The Epoch) in the early 1860s, he attempted first to steer a moderate course of national reconciliation through the furious political debates of the post-reform years. He then used those same platforms to express his increasingly bitter antipathy to the rationalism, atheism and vulgar materialism of the young radical intellectuals of the 1860s – the 'nihilists', as Turgenev termed them, led by the journalist-philosophers N. G. Chernyshevsky and N. A. Dobrolyubov. Throughout his journalistic career, but especially in *The Diary of a Writer* (1873–81), that crucible in which the material of his last novels, *A Raw Youth* and *The Brothers Karamazov*, was forged, Dostoyevsky consistently held up the Russian peasant as a moral ideal to which the intellectual might aspire. His 'populism', though, had little in common with that political idealisation of the 'socialist instincts' of the Russian people characteristic of members of the progressive intelligentsia such as Alexander Herzen and the Russian *narodniki* (populists). Instead, Dostoyevsky stressed the etymological link between the Russian words for 'peasant' (*krest'yanin*) and 'christian' (*khristianin*), and held that the simple Russian man preserved in his moral make-up, practices and institutions those elements of religiosity, native culture and communal life from which the Russian intellectual classes had been alienated by their assimilation of western reason, civilisation, and political thought. The westernised intellectual, for all his learning and material advantages, was a spiritual vagabond, denied real understanding by those very processes of understanding he had chosen to adopt. In this sense, as in many others, Dostoyevsky was in agreement with the Slavophiles, who in the great debates of the 1840s with their opponents the Westernisers had rejected the attempts of Peter the Great and Catherine the Great to force Russia into a Western European mould and had advocated a specifically religious culture and a uniquely Slavonic line of historical development. Dostoyevsky's views on the narrowness of Western man and the superiority of the apparently naive and unsophisticated Russian 'type' found their most compelling expression in his speech at the unveiling of a memorial in Moscow to the great Russian poet, A.S. Pushkin, in June 1880. The Pushkin Speech, like *The Brothers Karamazov* to which it is indissolubly linked, crowned a lifetime's reflection and allowed Dostoyevsky to reaffirm his admiration for Pushkin, whom he regarded as the most perfect embodiment of Russian national consciousness. In it he chided Russia's uprooted intellectuals for their spiritual bankruptcy and alienation from the living source of wisdom in the Russian people. It was to precisely this alienation that all Russia's contemporary ills, in particular the spread of socialism and revolution and the enmity between social classes, could be ascribed. Dostoyevsky urged the Russian westernised intellectual to 'humble himself' and to merge with the Russian people in the name of universalism and brotherhood.

These ideas may be traced back to Dostoyevsky's articles in *Vremya* in the 1860s and his advocacy, along with A.A. Grigoryev, of a 'cult of the soil' (*pochvennichestvo*). They also underlie his sustained polemic with Chernyshevsky and the other 'men of the 1860s' over the essential nature of man.

Following the death of Nicholas I in 1855, Russian intellectual life was reinvigorated after the enforced intellectual conformity and passivity of the old regime. A new generation of social and political thinkers, led by Chernyshevsky, impatiently brushed aside the naive and vapid idealism of their 'fathers', the generation of the 1840s, and proclaimed a new and radical realism that sought to approach man and the moral, social, political, and aesthetic problems confronting him in a rigidly rational and 'scientific' manner. In works such as *The Anthropological Principle in Philosophy* (1860) and his novel *What is to be Done?* (1863), Chernyshevsky rejected metaphysics and affirmed that man is governed by material needs and the rational desire to gratify these. A rational social order was thus one which allowed the greatest number to achieve the most self-interest. Dostoyevsky could not accept Chernyshevsky's rejection of dualism in human nature or his insistence that all man's actions could be rationally deduced from natural self-interest. Chernyshevsky's doctrine of 'rational egoism' threatened to reduce man to a mere series of conditioned reflexes and chemical reactions. His views did not allow for the presence of the metaphysical in nature or in man and they thus precluded the salvation which, in Dostoyevsky's view, only a religious consciousness could offer.

Dostoyevsky's ideas on human nature, on the bankruptcy of reason and materialism, on the superiority of the Russian people and the need for a specifically religious culture were not confined to his journalistic writings. The series of great novels which he began soon after his return from Siberia confirmed his religious rebirth. In *Notes from Underground* (1864) he sought to expose the absurdity of rational egoism by affirming the crucial role of the irrational as a spring of human behaviour. His protagonist, the Underground Man, may be seen as the first Existentialist hero in his vigorous attempts to preserve moral freedom and personal choice in the face of the threats posed by reason, contingency and self-interest. He deliberately acts against his own self-interest, spurning both reason and the laws of nature, in order to assert his independence. Dostoyevsky recognised that there was a danger too in such wilful rebellion, and his hero's revolt subsides into egoism, petty petulance and Hamlet-like inertia as he tries to avoid defining himself through his actions. We leave him simpering in his underground world, a valid reproach to Chernyshevsky's view of a rational humanity, but possessed of a sterile freedom which he cannot exercise. Dostoyevsky did not intend to offer his hero or the underground as worthy alternatives to reason. Instead he hoped to show his hero's recognition of the need for Christ, but this design was frustrated by the censor. 'That swine of a censor.' Dostoyevsky wrote to his brother in March 1864. 'The passages where I jeered at everything and sometimes blasphemed *for form's sake* he let through, but he suppressed the place where from all this I deduced the need for faith and Christ' (XXVIII/2, 73).

The need for faith and Christ is something which the hero of Dostoyevsky's next novel, *Crime and Punishment* (1866), also comes to recognise. Raskolnikov is a young student imbued with the materialism of the 1860s, who attempts to devise a rational, utilitarian morality that will justify the murder of a useless old pawnbroker who feeds off the misfortunes of others. Through his crime and the doubts that assail him afterwards Raskolnikov is forced to the realisation that a moral system grounded only in man's intellect and notions of utility is more likely to lead to violence, disintegration and despair than to a harmonious social order. He discovers a sense of true morality in the hidden irrational depths of his soul as he strives to come to terms with his actions. Under the influence of the meek, Christian prostitute, Sonya, he embarks upon the path of suffering which will lead to his salvation.

The Idiot (1868) affords Dostoyevsky the possibility of bringing his ideal of 'the positively good man' into conflict with a society riddled with the vices of a godless age, where money, materialism, egoism and calculation effectively disallow all true brotherhood and harmony. Prince Myshkin is presented as a Christ-like figure adrift in an apocalyptic setting, his trust in beauty, love and compassion sadly out of place in a nineteenth-century Babylon. If Dostoyevsky's sense of artistic truth insisted that his hero must fail, then this was in no way to detract from the validity of the ideals he embodied. The 'positively good man' is reduced to idiocy, but it is the world that is rotten, not he.

This vision of a world rotten to the core and inhabited by demons forms the heart of *The Devils* (1871–2), Dostoyevsky's most stridently anti-nihilist novel. The work's bitter parody of socialism and political revolutionaries is only one aspect of its call for a return to spiritual values. Its central character, Stavrogin, represents the void left when man's soul has been consumed by the false Western values of egoism, artificiality and atheism. Like the Underground Man, he is the victim of a craving for personal freedom that leaves him hopelessly alienated and incapable of any act apart from suicide. Crushed by the burden of freedom without moral responsibility, he takes his own life in a moment of profound ennui. Only the old Westerniser, Stepan Trofimovich Verkhovensky, finds salvation by abandoning his past and discovering the Russian people.

The moral collapse of a contemporary society which has abandoned God in favour of the material and intellectual gifts of Western civilisation is explored in *A Raw Youth* (1875) through the metaphor of a disintegrating, 'haphazard' family, whose members are no longer united by bonds of love. The illegitimate Arkady Dolgoruky's quest for his father becomes a quest for wholeness and 'harmony' (*blagoobraziye*) in the face of contemporary 'chaos' (*bezobraziye*). The fact that he finds this ideal not in his natural father, the Westernised and ultimately empty Versilov, but in the man who has raised him since childhood, the simple Russian peasant Makar Dolgoruky, effectively illustrates the central tenets of Dostoyevsky's moral vision.

Dostoyevsky's major novels before *The Brothers Karamazov* thus reveal his profound sense of the discordant, fragmented and unstable nature of contemporary reality and his recognition of the need for new religious harmonies to replace the delusive rational harmonies of Western civilisation. His character Lebedev in *The Idiot* had expressed this idea perfectly when he spoke of contemporary society's lack of 'a binding idea', some core of moral certainty around which man's life could coalesce. In the notebooks for *A Raw Youth* Dostoyevsky had confirmed Lebedev's diagnosis: 'There are no bases to our society ... One colossal quake and the whole lot will come to an end, collapse, and be negated as though it had never existed. And this is not just outwardly true ... but inwardly, morally so' (XVI, 329). It was against this background of perceived cultural collapse that Dostoyevsky wrote *The Brothers Karamazov* as an affirmation of man's need for God. The work was conceived by its author as nothing less than a 'civic deed', transcending mimetic art and the mere exposure of reality and devoted to the complete rout of those forces which had brought humanity to the verge of catastrophe. As he remarked after his Pushkin Speech in June 1880: 'The main thing about me they don't understand. They extol me for not being satisfied with the present political state of our country, but they don't see that I am showing them the way to the church' (cited in Magarshack, *The Brothers Karamazov*, p. xxiii).

By the early 1870s Dostoyevsky's personal and social circumstances had also changed. His second marriage to Anna Grigoryevna Snitkina, the young stenographer who had helped him meet the deadline for his novel, *The Gambler* (1866), had inaugurated a period of relative tranquillity, financial stability and domestic harmony which endured until his death. After their return from Europe in 1871 the Dostoyevskys had taken an apartment in St Petersburg and, from 1872, a summer house in the small town of Staraya Russa, where the writer was able to work without distraction. Staraya Russa was to serve as a model for the town of Skotoprigonyevsk in *The Brothers Karamazov*. Both officially and unofficially, Dostoyevsky's stature in Russia was now very considerable. To his readers, and to the younger generation in particular, he was a political martyr, an ex-political prisoner, whose novels, despite their increasingly anti-radical stance, had touched the nerve of Russian life, championed the ordinary Russian, and probed the hidden restlessness and moral aspirations of contemporary man. To many he was no less than a prophet, and his daily

routine in St Petersburg was constantly interrupted by corre-
spondents and callers seeking advice and guidance on a variety
of problems. To the Russian ruling circles this erstwhile political
opponent was now a powerful ally in the cause of Russian
conservatism, even though he remained under covert police
surveillance until the summer of 1875. Dostoyevsky's repudia-
tion of his revolutionary past, his consistent stance against
the radicals and his advocacy of traditional Russian values
inevitably brought him to the attention of those whose task it
was to stem the revolutionary tide which, in a wave of underground plotting and political assassinations, threatened to
engulf the tsarist regime in the decades following the half-
hearted political reforms of 1861.

At the beginning of the 1870s Dostoyevsky was introduced
by his friends Nikolay Strakhov and Apollon Maykov to Prince
V. P. Meshchersky, an influential Russian conservative responsible for the publication of a reactionary periodical, *Grazhdanin*
(The Citizen). So impressed was Meshchersky by Dostoyevsky's
views that he invited him to assume the editorship of *Grazhdanin*
at the end of 1872. Dostoyevsky performed this task diligently
throughout 1873 and the early part of 1874, even serving a
brief prison sentence in March 1874 for the periodical's in-
discretions. But he had grave misgivings about acting as a
mouthpiece for Meshchersky's crude political programmes and
instead attempted to give the periodical a more personal flavour.
This he did by publishing in it the early entries of *The Diary
of a Writer*, in which he commented on the major political,
literary and social issues of the day, and which attracted a
wide and attentive readership. When Dostoyevsky resigned the
editorship, he continued *The Diary of a Writer* as a separate
publication; as well as in 1873, it appeared in the years 1876,
1877, 1880 and 1881. This unique work served as a test bed for
the material explored in *The Brothers Karamazov* and other late
works. Through its distinctive informal structure Dostoyevsky
analysed the texture of contemporary Russian life, dwelling on
social themes which interested him, such as the maltreatment
of children and the growth in the incidence of suicides. He
also commented on political issues, such as Russia's support

for the Balkan Slavs, a cause which had his complete support, and continued to express his views on the moral degeneracy of contemporary life and the essential incompatibility of socialism and Christianity.

It was through Meshchersky that Dostoyevsky met Konstantin P. Pobedonostsev, then a member of the Senate close to the Royal Family, who as head of the Holy Synod was to become the architect of Russian reaction and a vigilant scourge of intellectual nonconformity in the reign of Alexander III. Dostoyevsky became a regular visitor to Pobedonostsev's Saturday soirées, enjoying his intellectual companionship and admiring many of his opinions. 'He has an enormous mind,' Dostoyevsky wrote of him in 1876. Pobedonostsev brought Dostoyevsky much official recognition and an introduction into high state and court circles. The two men possessed strikingly different personalities, but they shared much common ground in their attitudes to Russian and European social and religious problems in the 1870s. Both saw Western Europe and Europeanised Russia as enduring a process of moral and spiritual decline and fragmentation, which could be arrested only by submission to paternalistic autocracy and the teachings of the Russian Orthodox Church. Both objected to the extreme individualism which threatened the integrity of Westernised societies and both spurned the political solutions offered by democratic government and socialism. Despite their ideological closeness, there is real doubt as to whether Pobedonostsev specifically 'influenced' Dostoyevsky's thought, notwithstanding his claim that the section of *The Brothers Karamazov* called 'A Russian Monk' was written under his instructions and guidance. However, Pobedonostsev did supply Dostoyevsky with opinions and newspaper cuttings on a variety of matters treated in the novel, most especially on the question of trial by jury. Pobedonostsev had been officially involved in the drafting of the major judicial reform of 1864 which had introduced trial by jury, but by the 1870s he had real doubts about the leniency of courts anxious to appear 'enlightened' and the incompetence of juries faced by the eloquence of unscrupulous lawyers. It seems likely that Dostoyevsky's own doubts about legal procedures and his depiction in *The Brothers Karamazov* of a miscarriage of justice at the trial of Dmitry were confirmed by the views of Pobedonostsev.

However, Dostoyevsky had also witnessed the procedures of the new courts at the trial of the terrorist Vera Zasulich in the spring of 1878. Zasulich was charged with the attempted assassination of the despotic Governor of St Petersburg, General Trepov, in January 1878 and her trial evoked widespread interest throughout Europe. Dostoyevsky followed it with alarmed fascination for the light it shed both on the ideals of Russia's revolutionary youth and on the humanitarian credentials of the Russian government. He reacted to the outcome − Zasulich was acquitted − with profound ambiguity. The young defendant's zeal and idealism moved him deeply at a time in his life when he was prone to recall his own early radicalism and friendship with the critic Vissarion Belinsky. On the other hand, Zasulich's attempt on the life of Trepov struck Dostoyevsky as yet another twist in a spiral of political assassinations during the 1870s. Revolutionary activity had grown rapidly in Russia throughout the decade. Under the influence of Mikhail Bakunin, a wing of the *narodnik* (populist) movement had abandoned the peaceful path to social improvement in favour of direct insurrectionary activity. In December 1876 the revolutionary organisation *Zemlya i volya* (Land and Liberty) had organised a mass demonstration outside the Kazan Cathedral in Petersburg and in 1879 the radicals, having broken formally with the moderates and now under the banner of a new society, *Narodnaya volya* (The People's Will), passed a sentence of death on Alexander II. Attempts were made on the Tsar's life in April 1879 and February 1880, before he was finally assassinated in 1881, shortly after Dostoyevsky's death. Other leading government figures were also targeted.

Dostoyevsky, of course, was profoundly opposed to both the political ideals and the murderous methods of the terrorists. The fact that he began his work on *The Brothers Karamazov* in the summer of 1878, so soon after the trial of Zasulich, suggests that he found in the idea of regicide a vivid and suggestive metaphor for the themes he wished to explore in his novel. *The Brothers Karamazov*, like the earlier novels, is centred on the tragedy of moral and cultural collapse. In his final novel Dostoyevsky chose to approach this great question through the themes of parricide, the mutual responsibilities of fathers and children, and, as in *A Raw Youth*, the collapse of the family. As early as April 1876 he wrote that he was planning a 'very big novel' on important current issues and that 'for me one of the most important problems of the current moment ... is that of the younger generation, along with that of the contemporary Russian family, which I sense is no longer what it was twenty years ago' (XXIX/2, 78). The death sentence passed by representatives of the younger generation upon the father-Tsar (the word *batyushka* 'father' was commonly applied to the Tsar by the Russian people) invested Dostoyevsky's perception of the fragmentation of the family with an additional political significance, and it is interesting in this respect that the Russian critic L. P. Grossman should suggest that a prototype for Alyosha Karamazov was the student Dmitry Karakozov who in 1866 attempted to assassinate Alexander II, an event which shook Dostoyevsky profoundly. Grossman also quotes Suvorin's assertion that Dostoyevsky intended to continue his novel with Alyosha as a revolutionary who commits a political crime (*Dostoevsky*). The theme of parricide in *The Brothers Karamazov* thus binds several of Dostoyevsky's deepest fears into an evocative symbol of the catastrophic fragmentation of contemporary Russian life: in their moral confusion sons turn against fathers, fathers fail their sons, subjects turn against Tsar, and man abandons faith and rejects God, his divine father.

The relationship between fathers and children was one which exercised Dostoyevsky constantly in the 1870s. His own father had died in suspicious circumstances in 1839, although recent studies have cast doubt over the traditional view that he was murdered by his serfs. What is certain is that his father's death lay like a shadow over the rest of Dostoyevsky's life, compelling him to question the nature of his feelings for a possibly unlovable father, and stirring sensations of filial guilt and responsibility. When in *The Brothers Karamazov* Ivan knowingly paves the way for his father's murder by taking himself off to the village of Chermashnya, a barely disguised echo of Cheremoshna, where Dostoyevsky's father met his death, we sense the author's acute awareness of the events of forty years earlier.

If Dostoyevsky felt guilty as a son, he felt no less so as a father (Peace, *Dostoyevsky: An Examination*). In May 1878 his beloved son Alyosha died after an epileptic seizure, a disease inherited from his father. The author was inconsolable and his grief contributed to the tenderness with which he portrayed his young hero, Alyosha, and the other children in *The Brothers Karamazov*. For some time Dostoyevsky had been planning a novel about children as a token of his conviction that they represented all hopes for the future. His notebooks of the 1870s, as well as the pages of *The Diary of a Writer*, are filled with observations, particularly on the corruption and maltreatment of innocent children. His private correspondence also touches on the 'humanising' power of children and offers practical advice on their upbringing. In particular a letter of 27 March 1878 to an unidentified mother raises the following possibility:

Imagine that your child, having reached the age of 15 or 16, comes up to you (under the influence, for example, of malicious friends at school) and asks you or his father the following question: 'Why should I love you and why should this be an obligation?' Believe me, if this happens none of your knowledge or questions will help and you will have absolutely no answer for him. Therefore you must ensure that *he never comes to you* with such a question. And this will only be possible if he loves you directly and spontaneously, so that there is no way the question can enter his head ... (XXX/1, 17)

This letter prefigures Dostoyevsky's conviction in *The Brothers Karamazov* that mankind is a huge family which, like the domestic family, functions properly only when each is responsible for all, when a parent's love for a child — or, indeed, a Tsar's for his subjects — is, like God's, unconditional and when the question 'Why should I love you?' need not be asked of parent, monarch or God. It is through the adult maltreatment of children and the subsequent posing of this fatal question —

by the Karamazov sons to their father, by socialists to the tsarist order, and by Ivan Karamazov to God — that *The Brothers Karamazov* approaches what Mochulsky calls the 'world tragedy' of a catastrophically fragmented humanity (*Dostoevsky: His Life*).

Although *The Brothers Karamazov* was written in the late 1870s, it is set a decade earlier. In this respect it is, like *Crime and Punishment, The Idiot*, and *The Devils*, an anti-nihilist novel of the 1860s. This dislocation of the time of action from the time of writing, unique among his major works, allowed Dostoyevsky to break out of the novel's strict temporal co-ordinates and to invest his picture of the 1860s with attitudes and influences acquired in the final years of his life. In the other direction, too, *The Brothers Karamazov* outgrew its decade, drawing ideas, prototypes and reminiscences from Dostoyevsky's earlier life and work. The story of its conception and writing is a complex one and its origins lie in that reservoir of notebook ideas and fragments which also gave rise to the author's other great works of the late 1860s and 1870s. In December 1868, while at work on *The Idiot*, Dostoyevsky wrote to his friend Apollon Maykov, outlining a plan for a major work on a religious theme: 'I have in mind now ... a large novel to be called "Atheism" (for God's sake, this is between you and me), but before I start on it I shall have to read a whole library of atheists, catholics and orthodox' (XXVIII/2, 329). The work was to deal with a theme close to Dostoyevsky's heart: the loss of religious faith in the modern age. A quite ordinary middle-aged man suddenly, and for no apparent reason, loses his faith in God. This affects him dramatically and he plunges into a desperate search for life's meaning among the younger generation, atheists, Westernisers, Catholics, Jesuits, Poles, and even the Russian schismatic sects, before finding salvation and a new faith 'in Christ and the Russian soil, the Russian Christ and the Russian God'. Dostoyevsky confides to Maykov that he expects this to be his final work; and it is not difficult to discern in the project the same messianic spirit, the same desire to lead his countrymen to the Church, which lies behind *The Brothers Karamazov*, even if the details and character types of the later novel are not yet formed. By the beginning of 1870 Dostoyevsky was thinking along different lines, although he insisted to Maykov that this was essentially the same final great project:

The novel is to consist of five long tales ... (The general title of the novel is 'The Life of a Great Sinner', but each tale will have its own title). The main problem which informs all the parts is the one that has tormented me consciously or unconsciously all my life – the existence of God. The hero in the course of his life is an atheist, then a believer, then a fanatic and sectarian, then an atheist once more. The second tale is to take place in a monastery. This second tale carries all my hopes. Perhaps at last they will say that not everything I have written is trivial. (To you alone, Apollon Nikolayevich, I confess that I want to introduce Tikhon Zadonsky as the main figure of the second tale, under a different name, of course, but also a bishop in retreat in a monastery). A thirteen-year-old boy, who has taken part in the commission of a criminal offence, mature and depraved (I know the type), the future hero of the whole novel, is placed in the monastery by his parents ... This little wolf and child-nihilist meets up with Tikhon (Well, you know Tikhon's character and whole personality). I shall also place Chaadayev in this monastery (under a different name, of course). Why shouldn't Chaadayev spend a year in a monastery? ... Others could come to visit Chaadayev: Belinsky, for instance, or Granovsky, or even Pushkin ... But the main thing is Tikhon and the child.   (XXIX/1, 117–18)

Here for the first time Dostoyevsky's preoccupation with the existence of and need for God is combined with recognisable characters and motifs used in his final novel. Alyosha may be discerned in the boy, although at this stage his character is radically different; the introduction of the elder and wise man, Tikhon Zadonsky, anticipates the role of Zosima in the spiritual education of the youngest Karamazov. Tikhon had already appeared in the censored chapter of *The Devils*, 'Stavrogin's Confession'. The references to Peter Chaadayev (1793–1856), whose first *Philosophical Letter* (1836) had sent shock waves through Nicholaevan Russia with its vigorous pro-European condemnation of Russian history and the Orthodox church, are possibly taken up in the figure of Myusov in *The Brothers Karamazov*.

Dostoyevsky's other fragments and drafts of the period 1868—79 also contain many details and sketches that find their way into the finished novel. Some of these, such as the plan for a novel on the theme of fathers and children (1876), anticipate the general tenor of *The Brothers Karamazov*. Others relate much more specifically to the later work: a notebook entry written around the beginning of 1877, for example, makes specific reference to the Grand Inquisitor and Christ, while a list of works still to be tackled, dated 24 December 1877, reveals Dostoyevsky's intention to write 'a Russian Candide'. This latter suggests Voltairean elements in Ivan Karamazov's rebellion. The earliest of these more specific jottings bears the date 13 September 1874 and reveals the origins of Dostoyevsky's final novel in his own experiences:

Drama. In Tobolsk, about twenty years ago. Something like the Ilinsky episode. Two brothers, an old father, one of them has a fiancée with whom the second brother is secretly and enviously in love. But she loves the elder brother. But the elder brother, a young lieutenant, leads a debauched and merry life. He quarrels with his father. The father disappears. For several days there is no sign of him. The brothers discuss the inheritance. And suddenly the authorities arrive: they dig up the body from the cellar. The evidence points to the elder brother (the younger does not live with them). The elder brother is tried and sentenced to hard labour. (N.B. He quarrelled with his father, bragged about his mother's inheritance, and other stupid things ...) The evidence has been cleverly fabricated by the younger brother. The public is not sure who the murderer really is.
(XVII, 5)

The piece concludes with the younger brother's change of heart and confession some nineteen years later. All of this clearly foreshadows the miscarriage of justice when Dmitry Karamazov is convicted of the murder of his father and the real guilt lies with the younger brother. In *The Brothers Karamazov* Ivan is not of course the murderer, but it is his belief that 'all is permitted' which provides the ideological motivation for the real killer Smerdyakov. The details of this draft are, on Dostoyevsky's admission, taken from his own past. Whilst in prison in Omsk, he had met a retired lieutenant named Ilinsky who was serving a twenty-year term for the brutal murder of his father.

Dostoyevsky had described his case in the first chapter of his prison memoir *Notes from the House of the Dead*, where he had marvelled at Ilinsky's apparent lack of remorse. Later in *Notes from the House of the Dead* Dostoyevsky revealed that he had subsequently heard that Ilinsky was in fact innocent and had been released after wrongly serving ten years of his sentence.

The Ilinsky affair clearly contributed to Dostoyevsky's conception of Dmitry Karamazov, but the figure of the wrongly arrested parricide was not the only prototype for the eldest Karamazov son. While working on *The Brothers Karamazov* Dostoyevsky re-read Schiller's *Robbers*, which he had first seen performed as a boy of ten and which had exercised 'a very fruitful' influence on his subsequent spiritual development (XXX/1, 212). The play's themes of parricide and fraternal rivalry are identical with those of *The Brothers Karamazov*, and some of the features of the dissolute son Karl Moor are transferred to Dmitry. The influence of Schiller in fact informs the whole fabric of *The Brothers Karamazov* and is not confined merely to the supply of prototypes for Dostoyevsky's characters (Čiževskyj, 'Schiller und die *Brüder*').

It would seem that Dostoyevsky also created the figure of Ivan Karamazov with several real-life prototypes in mind. Anna Grigoryevna has suggested that he was partly modelled on the young philosopher Vladimir Solovyov, who was close to Dostoyevsky during his final years and who accompanied the writer to the Optina Pustyn monastery after the death of his son. Although Solovyov shared Ivan's intellectual sharpness and his concern over the relationship between church and state, he evolved a religious and metaphysical system far removed from Ivan's Euclidean rationalism. Indeed Solovyov has often been held up as the prototype for Alyosha Karamazov and his dreams of universal harmony. Belinsky, Herzen and Turgenev also played parts in the shaping of Ivan: Belinsky's rejection of a social harmony bought at the price of human suffering (see, for example, his letter of 1 March 1841 to V.P. Botkin) is uncannily similar to Ivan's rebellion and rejection of God's paradise, while Nina Perlina has painstakingly traced implied dialogue with the ideas of Herzen in Ivan's utterances ('Herzen in *The Brothers Karamazov*'). Victor Terras has convincingly demonstrated that Ivan's devil is ideologically and personally linked to Dostoyevsky's old enemy, the Westerniser and agnostic Turgenev ('Turgenev and the Devil').

Many other possible prototypes have been suggested for the major and minor characters of *The Brothers Karamazov* (Terras, *A Karamazov Companion*), and they clearly show how Dostoyevsky's last novel was rooted in the events, experiences and acquaintances of his life. But the absorption of such personal prototypes into the fictional matter of the novel is indirect and ultimately of little importance, for as Bakhtin first pointed out 'the prototypes found in Dostoyevsky's poetic world are not prototypes of characters, but prototypes of ideas' (Perlina, 'Herzen in *The Brothers Karamazov*'). In this respect the most significant sources of the characters in *The Brothers Karamazov* are to be found not among Dostoyevsky's friends and acquaintances, but among those earlier articulations of given ideological and moral positions, the characters of his previous novels. Thus, to cite but two examples, Alyosha Karamazov is clearly linked with the meekness and compassion of Sonya (in *Crime and Punishment*) and Myshkin (in *The Idiot*), while Ivan raises to new levels the revolt and egoism of Raskolnikov (in *Crime and Punishment*) and the hero of *Notes from Underground*.

This is the most important sense in which *The Brothers Karamazov* represents the summation and culmination of Dostoyevsky's career. It synthesises, refines and deepens the achievements of his earlier writings. It is therefore not surprising to learn that the actual working drafts for this final novel are relatively concise and contain little evidence of the monumental creative struggle which accompanied the birth of the earlier novels (Wasiolek, *Fyodor Dostoevsky: The Notebooks*). The whole of Dostoyevsky's previous life and work was the true workshop in which *The Brothers Karamazov* was forged.

Chapter 2

The novel

The family

Like Tolstoy's *Anna Karenina*, *The Brothers Karamazov* offers a picture of a Russian landowning family in the middle decades of the nineteenth century. There are, of course, differences of detail between the glittering urban life depicted by Tolstoy and the comparative simplicity of Dostoyevsky's provincial setting, but in a very fundamental sense these works are both novels *about* the family. Tolstoy makes this clear from his well-known opening sentence: 'All happy families are alike; each unhappy family is unhappy in its own way.' Yet this sentence does more than merely signal the novel's subsequent preoccupation with family life. In its clear attempt to generalise the nature of family happiness and to particularise unhappy families, it discloses, perhaps more by accident than by design, the essential nature of Tolstoy's view. All happy families are alike; unhappy families depart from this implied *norm* in an infinite variety of ways. The concept of the normal family, indeed of normality in general, informs the whole of Tolstoy's moral vision. His work, like his vision, is in an important sense profoundly centripetal: life in its particular aspects might depart from, but in general it returns to, an indisputably stable core of normality. Sexuality and infidelity destroy Anna's family and poison her relationship with her child, but her experience is balanced by that of others: her brother's marriage survives his adultery, and that of Kitty and Levin forms a basis for the ideal of family happiness. Tolstoy, in this novel as in others, uses a range of secondary characters and subsidiary resources to dissipate the particular effects of abnormality. Like the surface of a pond into which a stone has been cast, the stuff of the Tolstoyan novel recovers its equilibrium and returns to normality. The enduring effect of *War and Peace*, for example, is created not by the huge, historically disruptive events of the Napoleonic wars, but by the stability and traditional values inherent in the Rostov family.

Dostoyevsky did not share Tolstoy's profound confidence in the enduring powers of normality. Indeed, normality is conspicuously absent from his works. The moral and social vision disclosed by his novels is deeply centrifugal; the world he saw around him was fragmented, shifting, unstable and disordered. In his notebooks for *A Raw Youth* he described a programme for that novel which just as effectively set out the aims of *The Brothers Karamazov*:

The title of the novel: 'Disorder'.
The whole idea of the work is to affirm the notion of universal disorder, to show that this disorder is all over the place, in society, in its affairs, in its governing principles (which for this very reason do not exist), and in the decay of the idea of the family. If passionate convictions still exist, then they are destructive ones (socialism). Moral ideas no longer exist, suddenly not a single one remains ...
(XVI, 80–1)

In a letter of 1854 Dostoyevsky described himself as 'a child of the age' and went on to define that age as one of 'uncertainty' (*neveriye*) and 'doubt' (*somneniye*) (XXVIII, 176). What he meant by this was to be clarified many times over in his subsequent artistic and journalistic writings: Europe and Europeanised Russia, in the wake of the age of revolutions, of burgeoning capitalism and the disintegration of the established social, moral, political and psychological order, was in the throes of a process of profound cultural transformation. In *The Diary of a Writer* for 1877 Dostoyevsky describes how in Russia the old landowning order is undergoing 'some new, still unknown, but radical change ... some enormous regeneration into novel, still latent, almost utterly unknown forms' (XXV, 35). The entry deals with the suicide of a twelve-year-old schoolboy, but it goes on to speculate that such an event would not have occurred in the settled and structured order of the landowning family life described by Tolstoy. The firm basis imparted to existence by that order would have prevented the suicide. But, says Dostoyevsky, contemporary life is distinguished by chaos, in which a 'normal law and guiding thread' has not yet been discovered, and which leads to general decomposition and the disintegration of family bonds. It was for some new artist 'of Shakespearian magnitude' to discover the new laws and guiding thread behind contemporary life, but in the meantime the present was 'a thunderous age, filled with so many colossal, staggering and quickly shifting events' (XXV, 193).

In *The Diary of a Writer* Dostoyevsky repeatedly refers to Tolstoy as the *historian* of the old landowning order. The implication is clear: even when they are set in the present, Tolstoy's novels, with their confidence in the power of normality to reassert itself, are tantamount to historical pictures of a vanishing world. Despite their descriptive trappings and preoccupation with the physical details of life, they fail in what was for Dostoyevsky the primary objective of realistic art — the elucidation of the underlying 'essence of reality' (XXIX/I, 19), that is, its disorder and instability. In the final chapter of *A Raw Youth* Nikolay Semyonovich, in whose family the hero had lived while at school, comments wryly that he would not like to be the chronicler of contemporary reality, 'a thankless task lacking beautiful forms'. Instead, he continues, 'if I were a Russian novelist and possessed talent, I would without fail take my heroes from the Russian hereditary nobility, for only in that type of cultured Russian person can you find even the appearance of fine order ...' (XIII, 453). Such a novel would be a historical work, but, in a barely disguised reference to Tolstoy, Nikolay warns:

It is possible so to distract the reader that he will accept a historical picture for one still possible in our time. Such a work of art, if executed by a great talent, would no longer belong in the province of Russian literature so much as in the realm of Russian history. It would be an artistically complete picture of a Russian mirage, but appearing real as long as you don't realise that it is a mirage. (XIII, 454)

It was through such polemics with Tolstoy that Dostoyevsky refined the programme for his own last novel. Just as the author of *Anna Karenina* had found in the Russian landowning family a metaphor for his faith in normality, so did Dostoyevsky see in the disintegration of that family a microcosm of a more general cultural collapse. He had signalled his interest in *The Diary of a Writer* for January 1876, where he wrote: 'I have always observed children, but now I am paying them particular attention. I long ago set myself the ideal of writing a novel about present-day Russian children and of course their present-day fathers, in their present-day mutual interrelation' (XXII, 7). Such children are 'the cast-offs of society, "accidental" members of "accidental" families'. The concept of the 'accidental' family, where normal bonds of love and mutual responsibility no longer exist, is crucial to Dostoyevsky's understanding of the relationship between fathers and children in the contemporary age. The motif recurs in *A Raw Youth* and is repeated later in *The Diary of a Writer*, where it implies a clear rejection of Tolstoy's view of familial stability:

Never has the Russian family been more shaken loose, more degraded, more unsorted and unformed than now. Where will you now find such 'Childhoods and boyhoods' as have been depicted so harmoniously and graphically by Count Leo Tolstoy as representations of *his* epoch and his family, or those shown in his *War and Peace?* ... What is this *accidental* quality and what do I understand by the term? ... In my view the accidental quality of the modern Russian family consists in the loss by present-day fathers of a general idea with regard to their families, an idea common to all fathers, which would bind them together, in which they could themselves believe, and which they could teach their children to believe, passing on to them this faith in life ... The very presence of such a general idea binding together society and the family is already the beginning of order, i.e. moral order ... In our age there is no such order, since there is nothing general or binding. (XXV, 173, 178–9)

Dostoyevsky's view that the fragmentation of the family is symptomatic of, and largely responsible for, the loss of a binding moral idea in contemporary society is carried in its entirety into *The Brothers Karamazov*. In a move characteristic of the way he distributes his own convictions among different and apparently inappropriate characters in his fiction, Dostoyevsky allows the Public Prosecutor at Dmitry's trial to employ his own views on the moral decline of Russian society

and the Russian family as the basis for securing a false end —
the conviction of an innocent man. The Prosecutor attributes
the murder of Fyodor Pavlovich and the general indifference
to such crimes among so-called progressive thinkers to a widespread cynicism and moral exhaustion evident in the younger
generation, whose moral principles are shattered to their very
foundations. This in turn he attributes to the failure of the
family principle, so clearly illustrated in the Karamazov family.
Fyodor Pavlovich, 'one of our present-day fathers', has lost all
sense of a binding idea and of a father's spiritual responsibility
to transmit to his children something positive and beautiful.
Instead, on the principle of 'après moi le déluge' he has sacri-
ficed all social and paternal duty in favour of cynicism and
sensualism. His sons in turn, sensing themselves relieved of
all filial obligations by his behaviour, reduce family bonds
to those of utility alone by asking why they should love their
father: 'But if parricide is merely a prejudice', continues the
Prosecutor, 'and if every child is to ask of his father, "Father,
why should I love you?", then what will become of us, what
will become of the foundations of society?' (Book XII, Ch. 14).

The Prosecutor's view of the Karamazov family is, of course,
clouded by his conviction that Dmitry is guilty of the murder
of his father. Despite this, however, his suggestion that the
Karamazovs are symptomatic of a contemporary malaise is
clearly shared by Dostoyevsky. The Karamazov family relation-
ships are invested with a symbolism designed to imply a breakdown in the transmission of values and mutual responsibility
between the generations. Fyodor Pavlovich's withholding of
Dmitry's inheritance and the resentment this engenders in the
son are richly suggestive, for it is more than money that is at
stake here. It is the whole legitimacy of the father-son relationship, a legitimacy already thrown into question by the ease
with which Fyodor Pavlovich forgot the existence of his eldest
son immediately after his birth and with which he abandoned
him at the age of three years to the care of the family retainer,
Grigory Kutuzov. The younger sons fared little better; they
too were abandoned in childhood, first to Grigory and then
to relatives of old Karamazov's second wife, and their father

subsequently accepted no responsibility for their well-being or education. It is precisely such parental failure that allows Ivan in turn to articulate the dark thought: 'Who does not desire the death of his father?' This idea haunts his brothers, informs the whole novel and clearly underpins the theme of parricide, that final affirmation of the abnormality of this family. The diseased Karamazov family with its poisoned generational ties is starkly contrasted with the relationship between the retired officer Snegiryov and his son, Ilyusha. Despite material poverty and Ilyusha's mortal illness, the relationship between father and son is demonstrably alive in the plans they hatch together, in the father's inconsolable grief at the loss of his son, and in little Ilyusha's brave determination to stand up for his father when the latter is subjected to Dmitry's assault and the mockery of the other children (Book IV, Chs. 6–7).

At the heart of the Karamazov family lies the stain of illegitimacy, and this allows Dostoyevsky to develop another, darker symbol: that of the bastard son, Pavel Fyodorovich Smerdyakov, whose name and patronymic grotesquely invert those of his natural father and whose given surname, implying a stinking abomination, suggests the corruption running through the family. The fact that it is Smerdyakov who actually commits the murder of Fyodor Pavlovich is thus richly symbolic, reinforcing the links that have been established between illegitimacy and parricide.

Of all the Karamazovs only Dostoyevsky's chosen 'hero', the youngest son Alyosha, retains a sense of family and of generational ties. Initially this is suggested through his memories of his mother, in a scene which Dostoyevsky invests with mystical and religious significance. She is surrounded in Alyosha's memory by icons and lamps, and is bathed in the slanting rays of the setting summer sun, an image which always carried a strong emotive charge in Dostoyevsky's writings. The significance of the passage is suggested in Alyosha's sense that it is 'just as though she were standing alive before me' (Book I, Ch. 4). Filial love not only binds together generations, but also rescues the departed from the oblivion of death.

This latter idea is further suggested when Alyosha seeks out his mother's grave, the whereabouts of which is unknown to his father: 'Fyodor Pavlovich could not show him where he had buried his second wife, since he had never visited her grave after her coffin had been covered, and it had been so long ago that he had entirely forgotten where she had been buried' (Book I, Ch. 4). In Russian there is an etymological link between 'to bury' (*khoronit'*) and 'to preserve' (*khranit'*), so that Fyodor Pavlovich's ignorance of the whereabouts of his wife's grave is doubly suggestive of his failure as a father to preserve family values and transmit them to succeeding generations. Significantly it is the servant Grigory, who assumed paternal responsibility for the Karamazov children, who does remember the whereabouts of Alyosha's mother's grave and indeed has tended it constantly.

It is clear that Alyosha's sense of the family is not acquired from his own father. There is another symbol of fatherhood that plays a larger part in Alyosha's spiritual development and is important for the novel as a whole: the institution of the monastic Elder. Father Zosima assumes the role of father which Fyodor Pavlovich has renounced. In a chapter which is tantamount to a discourse on the significance of the institution of Elders, Dostoyevsky writes:

What, then, is an Elder? An Elder is someone who takes your soul and your will into his soul and will. On choosing an Elder you renounce your own will and yield it to him in complete submission and self-abnegation ... The obligations due to an Elder are not the same as ordinary 'obedience', which has always existed in our monasteries. They affirm the eternal willingness of those who follow the Elder to confess to him, and the indestructible bond between Elder and disciples.   (Book I, Ch. 5)

In this way Dostoyevsky suggests the institution of Elders as a model of the ideal family structure, in which isolation and fragmentation may be overcome, individualism absorbed into responsibility for others, and the seed sown for 'the moral regeneration of man from slavery to freedom and for moral perfectibility'.

The views expressed by Dostoyevsky in *The Brothers*

Karamazov on the significance of the family, the loss of a binding idea in contemporary life, the need for fathers to transmit values to their children, the responsibilities of children to unite in filial love for the preservation of their fathers, all accord with a distinctive philosophical system devised by the remarkable nineteenth-century Russian mystic, Nikolay Fyodorov, whose ideas Dostoyevsky first encountered in 1876. Fyodorov (1828–1903) was eccentric by any standards. The illegitimate son of Prince P. I. Gagarin, he nevertheless received a full education and worked for several years as a provincial schoolteacher before embarking in 1868 upon a career as librarian at the Rumyantsev Library (now the Lenin Library) in Moscow. Erudite, visionary and profoundly ascetic, he eschewed all manifestations of individualism, even refusing to publish his thought under his own name. It was left to others to collate his voluminous papers and publish them after his death under the title of *Philosophy of the Common Task* (1906). The philosophical system that emerges from this distinctive work is a startling mixture of supernatural nonsense, naive utopianism and prophetic glimpses of the opportunities afforded by scientific progress. Fyodorov's point of departure is a traditional one which posits the original organic unity of all creation, including man. However, this organism has been fragmented by the growth of individualism and isolation, a process illustrated in man's penchant for war, his self-interest, the Darwinian struggle for survival, the separation of knowledge and action, the contempt shown to past generations as they are swept aside in the name of forward progress, and the way in which the ideal of nationhood has come to be associated with the concept of 'statehood' (*gosudarstvennost'* – i.e. implying the primacy of artificial and mechanical political bonds), rather than with 'fatherlandness' (*otechestvennost'* – i.e. implying the primacy of organic tribal and generational bonds). The result is the current state of 'unrelatedness' (*nerodstvo*) and 'lack of brotherhood' (*nebratstvo*) characteristic of modern societies.

Fyodorov advocates a return to human brotherhood and the universal recognition of a 'common task' in the 'regulation'

and control of the blind forces of nature. This will begin with
the application of science to achieve such practical ends as
climate control and interplanetary colonisation, but it will
culminate in the 'union of the sons for the resurrection of
their fathers, as they become a relatedness, a *psychocracy*'
(*Sochineniya*, p. 65). The primary task of each generation is
not to discard previous ones in the headlong, 'unrelated' rush
into the future called progress, not to assert 'the superiority
of the living over the dead', but to recognise that the whole of
the earth is a graveyard from which the dead may be reclaimed
by common effort. Fyodorov thus envisages a mutual responsibility between present and past generations, 'a mutual turning
of the hearts of the fathers to the sons and of the sons to the
fathers' (p. 86):

The task of the fathers, the parents, ends with the upbringing of the
children; then begins the task of the sons, those who restore life.
In giving birth to and raising their children, the parents give up life
to them, while the task of resurrection begins with the returning of
life to the parents.   (p. 87)

That Dostoyevsky drew upon what he knew of Fyodorov's
ideas during his work on *The Brothers Karamazov* is clear from
his notebooks and drafts. In fragments relating to the first
part of the novel there may be found the following entries:

The resurrection of our ancestors. The landowner on Ilinsky: 'He
not only won't resurrect them, he'll even send them packing' ...

The resurrection of our ancestors depends on us.
About obligations to our kin. The Elder says that God gave us kin
so that through them we can learn *love* ...

Landowner: 'That one won't be resurrecting his ancestors'.
                                                    (XV, 203–8)

Moreover, the novel in its final form contains several
passages best understood in relation to Fyodorov's thought:
there is Alyosha's anxiety to know the whereabouts of his
mother's grave, already mentioned; there is his reply to Ivan's
comment that Europe is a graveyard and precious are the dead
that lie there: 'Why, raise up your dead, who have perhaps
never died at all!' (Book V, Ch. 3); there are observations by

both Father Zosima and his mysterious visitor about the destructive isolation characteristic of the present age and the loss of all sense of solidarity (Book VI, Ch. 2); there is the repetition throughout the novel of the motif that 'all are responsible'; and there is Alyosha's experience of the organic unity of all creation, of his soul coming into contact with other worlds, in the 'Cana of Galilee' episode (Book VII, Ch. 4).

Considerable critical controversy has been aroused by the question of whether Dostoyevsky, while working on *The Brothers Karamazov*, was influenced by Fyodorov's ideas or merely found in them confirmation of his own thought (see, for example, Linnér, *Starets Zosima*). Certainly he shared Fyodorov's belief in physical, rather than metaphorical, resurrection (XXX/I, 14). It is equally certain he did not agree that this could be accomplished through applied science. What is beyond dispute is that although Fyodorov's thought might not have shaped Dostoyevsky's ideas, it most obviously helped to determine the artistic expression of these ideas in his final novel. Fyodorov's philosophical ideal concentrates around a unified family structure where the sons are bound in brotherhood for the common task of the resurrection of their fathers. *The Brothers Karamazov* inverts this ideal by depicting a fragmented family, where each of the brothers is in his isolation responsible, not for the resurrection of his father, but for his murder.

The fragmented hero

The ideas of discord and fragmentation underlying Dostoyevsky's view both of the family and of reality as a whole are carried over into his depiction of the hero of *The Brothers Karamazov*, and in this respect the novel marks an apparent departure from its author's previous artistic practice. Many critics have commented on the essentially dramatic nature of Dostoyevsky's art, and on his tendency to construct his novels around a single central character and a single dramatic event (Ivanov, *Freedom and the Tragic Life*, Steiner, *Tolstoy or Dostoevsky*). This is most apparent in the great novels.

Raskolnikov and the murder of the pawnbroker are the twin centres of *Crime and Punishment*: the event dominates the novel's action and the hero's consciousness fills its space, to the exclusion of almost everything else. Prince Myshkin and the murder of Nastasya Filippovna perform similar functions in *The Idiot*: Nastasya's death at the end of the work is prefigured right from the start with all the inevitability of the classically tragic dénouement, and Myshkin's presence galvanises the lives of all the other characters. The murder of Shatov is central to the political intrigue of *The Devils*, while the enigmatic presence of Stavrogin is like a black hole warping the novel's whole gravitational field. Within these hero-centred artistic structures the secondary characters play clearly subsidiary roles. Unlike in the Tolstoyan novel, where the secondary characters broaden the range of vision and normalise the artistic reality by affording real alternatives to the central figures, Dostoyevsky's lesser figures tend to reflect and exaggerate the central hero. Like parodistic doubles they lack the quality of true 'otherness'. They thus compound the Dostoyevskian novel's specific concentration on its centre and thereby deepen its dramatic intensity.

These same structural principles are utilised again in *The Brothers Karamazov*, with one notable difference: the murder of Fyodor Pavlovich still provides a central dramatic focus for the action, but the role of central hero is now distributed among the three Karamazov sons. Yet, as we shall see, this move forms part of Dostoyevsky's *philosophical* design in the novel; it does not represent a genuine new departure from the *structural* norms employed in his earlier works. Taken together, the three brothers still perform the structural function of a single central hero, but separately they are designed to illustrate the fragmentation of the individual into the three aspects that make up his being: the mind, the body, and the soul. The cold, enigmatic Ivan discharges only ideas: he is a builder of systems, an inventor of paradox. For the most part he lacks both the emotional immediacy of Dmitry and the spirituality of Alyosha. His enthusiasm is confined largely to abstract concepts and dialectics, and the crisis he faces in the course of the novel is a crisis of reason. Dmitry possesses warmth, physical strength, and great emotional and sensual capacity, but these are uncontrolled by either an intellectual or a spiritual bridle. The crisis with which the events of the novel confront him is related to his physical nature. Finally, there is Alyosha, a novice seeking spiritual guidance in a monastery, who is apparently free of both the physicality and the intellectualism of his two brothers. He too undergoes a crisis in the course of the novel, and, significantly, this crisis is a spiritual one.

The three brothers are clearly intended to be viewed as a collective symbol of an organic whole — the unity of mind, body and soul — that has been catastrophically fragmented in modern man. This metaphorical interpretation is, of course, a partial one — it should not obscure the fact that Dostoyevsky's characters in this novel, as elsewhere, function equally successfully as convincing individual figures. But the metaphor of a fragmented collective hero takes us straight to the heart of Dostoyevsky's philosophy of man and of his epistemological thought. From the 1840s onwards Dostoyevsky's works had identified the problem of the disintegration of human nature, the atomisation of man's inner psychic essence, while his post-exile works had offered a more acute analysis of the problem and an explanation of its cause. The early works afford striking pictures of victims of a profound dualism, whose contradictory and self-destructive behaviour is the outcome of antagonistic and discordant inner forces such as reason and egoism, immediacy and consciousness. The works written after Dostoyevsky's return from exile, and following his first visit to Western Europe, clearly attribute this destructive fragmentation of man's psyche to the pernicious effects of European rationalism. The assertion of reason at the expense of man's other faculties of cognition, such as instinct, emotion and faith, both impoverishes and unbalances human existence, leading to moral confusion, disappointment, and even barbarism. Raskolnikov's murder of the pawnbroker, for example, is presented as the result of his attempt to implement an exclusively rational morality and to suppress other aspects of his moral self. His eventual recognition of the immorality of his crime and his conversion in Siberia mark his recapture of his total being and the reintegration of his personality.

In *The Diary of a Writer* for July–August 1877 Dostoyevsky hints at a source for his presentation of the fragmented hero in *The Brothers Karamazov*: 'In many ways my convictions are purely Slavophile, although I am not quite a Slavophile' (XXV, 195). Admittedly, this entry deals with the coincidence between Dostoyevsky's views and the social and political ideas of Slavophilism, but its title, 'The Confessions of a Slavophile', implies a more general sympathy with that thought. The Slavophiles were a rather loosely-knit group of Romantic nationalist philosophers who in the 1830s and 1840s elaborated a view of Russia's future based upon a return to the principles of the pre-Petrine period and a rejection of Western European cultural influences. Central to their thought was the ideal of 'the integral personality', an ideal preserved in Orthodox culture but destroyed by the cult of reason in Europe. In a famous essay of 1852, 'On the Nature of European Culture and its Relationship to Russian Culture', a leading Slavophile, Ivan Kireyevsky, had argued that classical paganism and the Roman influence in the West had led to a disproportionate emphasis placed there on human reason. This 'self-propelling scalpel of reason' had gradually excised man's other cognitive faculties, breaking down the 'integral totality' (*tsel'nost'*) of his personality, fostering intellectual autonomy, and thereby leading to progressive social disintegration. Western societies were thus at best artificial structures, in which the basic unit was the autonomous rational individual and where social cohesion could be achieved only by the force of external laws. Orthodox, pre-Petrine Russia had escaped these influences and its society had remained a unitary organism held together not by artificial external bonds but by inner moral law and the shared sense of 'communality' (*sobornost'*).

Despite his reservations about points of ideological detail, Dostoyevsky was in broad sympathy with the organicism inherent in Slavophile thought. The dispersal of a single 'integral personality' among the three Karamazov sons marked his acknowledgement of the psychic fragmentation of Europeanised man, which, like the dissolution of organic family bonds, was symptomatic of the disorder afflicting the educated sections of contemporary Russian society. The Karamazov family is tainted by the alien influences absorbed by Russian educated society after the Westernisation of Peter the Great. Its members lack both the psychological and the social coherence of the unspoiled Russian peasant and they are drawn inevitably not to familial unity, but into a darker and more tragic conspiracy — parricide. The fragments of personality represented by the Karamazov sons are all implicated in the murder of their father. Each of the brothers bears some responsibility for his death, and in each the nature of the responsibility is related to the dominant characteristic he embodies: Ivan's guilt is intellectual, Dmitry's physical and emotional, and Alyosha's spiritual. This variation on the novel's central theme that 'all are responsible' has been thoroughly discussed in the critical literature (see, for example, Peace, *Dostoevsky: An Examination*), but the outline of the argument must be examined again here.

Although it is Smerdyakov who actually commits the crime, it emerges in the course of the novel that he was consciously acting out theoretical premises articulated by Ivan. It is Ivan who at the trial affirms the existence of parricidal impulses as a widespread characteristic of the psyche of modern man. 'Who does not desire the death of his father?' he asks (Book VII, Ch. 5), and his own behaviour makes clear his distaste for Fyodor Pavlovich and indifference to the possibility of his murder. In his own mind this indifference is associated with the moment on the night before his departure when he coldly listened for his father's fearful movements in the room below. Moreover, it is Ivan who calculatingly ensnares Smerdyakov's limited intellect with the seductive doctrine that if God does not exist, then all is permitted. For the aspiring intellectual, Smerdyakov, such ideas are novel and inspirational, and they are not to be confined to the abstract wastes of the intellect. When allied to his innate immorality and sense of having been treated unjustly, they complete the motivation required to carry out the murder.

Ivan's complicity in the murder is confirmed in other details. His departure from the house and professed intention to visit the village of Chermashnya leave the way open for the murderer to act, and they provide a clear signal to Smerdyakov that Ivan is prepared to allow the murder of his father. His subsequent attempts to deny to himself the extent of his passive responsibility are confounded by an occurrence on the way to his third interview with Smerdyakov, which confronts Ivan with the same moral dilemma. He inadvertently knocks over a drunken peasant and leaves him to freeze in the snow, arguing that he cannot be held responsible for the peasant's death simply by not being there to look after him. It is symptomatic of Ivan's developing sense of moral responsibility that after the encounter with Smerdyakov, with its clear disclosure of the role he played in motivating the servant, he returns to tend to the fallen peasant (Book XI, Ch. 8).

Ivan's intellectual contribution to the tragedy of parricide is, moreover, enhanced and raised to genuinely religious levels in Book V, Ch. 4, 'Rebellion'. In one of the most famous and effective of all literary conversations Ivan reveals to his brother Alyosha the nature of his rebellion against God's universal order. His inability to accept an apparently irrational divine scheme that requires the sufferings of innocent children in the name of some future harmony leads him to return his ticket of admission to paradise and to turn against his heavenly father – whose existence he is prepared to acknowledge – in a gesture of profound religious rebellion. Ivan asks of God the same question raised by the Public Prosecutor at Dmitry's trial: 'Father, why should I love you?' And in the absence of a rationally satisfactory answer he turns his back on God, just as he also turns his back on his earthly father. Grotesque as the analogy might seem, both Fyodor Pavlovich and God serve to illustrate Ivan's rejection of an unlovable father.

Dmitry's guilt, on the other hand, is entirely emotional and physical. His brooding physical presence, emotional outbursts of hostility towards his father, and occasional acts of direct physical violence create an appropriate climate and widespread expectations of parricide. He is also guilty, as Peace puts it, 'of assaulting the very concept of fatherhood itself' (*Dostoyevsky: An Examination*). His self-control in drawing back from the murder of his biological father is marred by the severe blow he inflicts with the pestle upon the man who truly raised him, the retainer Grigory. His humiliation of little Ilyusha's father, Snegiryov, is not only a further assault on the concept of fatherhood but, more tellingly, an invasion of the family whose bonds of respect between father and son have been offered as a contrast to the fragmentation of the Karamazov family unit.

To complete the pattern, Alyosha's guilt is associated with the failure of faith. First he is enticed by his devious fellow novice Rakitin into admission of the fact that he does not trust Dmitry by suspecting that he, Dmitry, might really kill his father (Book II, Ch. 7). Secondly, the death and unseemly decomposition of Father Zosima provoke in Alyosha a temporary crisis and loss of faith in his divine father, God. This in turn distracts him from events in the Karamazov household and allows him to lose sight of two paternal requests which, had they been obeyed, might have prevented the crime: on the day before the murder Fyodor Pavlovich was insistent that Alyosha should be with him the following day, and Zosima, Alyosha's spiritual father, had earlier enjoined the novice to watch over his father and brother. What is more, the frailty of Alyosha's untested faith allows him to be drawn momentarily into complicity with Ivan's rebellion against God, as he admits that he too would have usurped God's right and demanded the death of a general who set his hounds on a child:

'Shoot him!' Alyosha muttered softly, raising his eyes to his brother with a pale, twisted sort of smile.
'Bravo!' Ivan yelled out with something like rapture. 'If you say so, then ... Ah, what a fine little monk you are! So that's the sort of little devil you have dwelling in your heart, Alyosha Karamazov!'
(Book V, Ch. 4)

As he recognises himself, Alyosha too is a victim of the fatal Karamazov nature.

Finally, Dostoyevsky suggests the collective Karamazov complicity in the tragedy of parricide through a network of implied personality linkages and correspondences between the brothers on the one hand and both the murderer and his victim on the other. The sensuality of Dmitry is clearly echoed in that of his father and highlighted by their being enthralled by the same woman, Grushenka. The same potential for sensuality is acknowledged in the nature of Alyosha. There is also a grotesque correspondence between Alyosha's disappointment when proof of Zosima's holiness fails to materialise on his death and Fyodor Pavlovich's comic assertion that he will believe in hell only if it can be demonstrated that it has a ceiling to support the hooks necessary for dragging down the sinners:

If there is no ceiling, then there can be no hooks. But if there are no hooks it means that all the rest is doubtful: who then will drag me down with hooks? And if they don't drag me down, then what will happen? Where would be the justice in the world? *Il faudrait les inventer* − the hooks that is, just for me.   (Book I, Ch. 4)

This passage affords an example of Dostoyevsky's finely judged use of humour. The mock *gravitas* with which Fyodor Pavlovich deploys his argument is entirely out of keeping with the absurdity of the argument itself. Moreover, the comically inappropriate references to justice and Voltaire, along with the mock-dialectical reasoning, establish a further link, this time with Ivan. Ivan too demands the same rationality of the divine order; he too shares the same concern for justice, and in the absence of it he mounts a rebellion against God which is later grossly echoed by Fyodor Pavlovich in a conversation with Alyosha:

As for your paradise, Alexey Fyodorovich, I want none of it, you should know that. Moreover, your paradise is no proper place for any decent fellow, even it it does exist.   (Book IV, Ch. 2)

Such overlapping and repetition of verbal and philosophical motifs, where the voice and beliefs of one character are parodistically heard in the speech of another, become a distinctive feature of *The Brothers Karamazov*, serving here to establish a character continuum and to bind all to the central symbol of parricide. The same technique is employed to tie the three brothers to Smerdyakov, the most compelling symbol of their collective guilt. The dark and disgusting Smerdyakov is a highly melodramatic and diabolical figure. If at times we cannot quite believe in him as a figure from reality, then this does not matter, for he is designed − along with many other features of the work − to enlarge the meaning of *The Brothers Karamazov* by leading us from the world of the nineteenth-century realistic novel into that of myth. Smerdyakov haunts both the novel and the minds of the brothers. He is their composite double, the agent of the dark side of their natures, a pledge of their complicity in the murder of their father. He stands before them like a hideously distorting mirror, reflecting their own failings in a fashion that compels recognition of the ugliness of these failings. For example, Ivan out of a sense of human dignity and pride concludes that if God does not exist or is rejected, then 'all is permitted'; human beings are their own masters, responsible for their own actions, and they should base their behaviour not on the promise of redemption or the threat of damnation in the afterlife, but on a morality of their own making founded upon the freedom of choice in the face of good and evil. For Ivan this is an idea of nobility, which liberates man from superstition and compels him to exercise his own moral discretion in a rational choice between good and evil. But Smerdyakov's behaviour is a travesty of this idea: he exposes its fallacy by using it as an excuse for murdering Ivan's (and his own) father. In this way Ivan is forced to recognise that the morality embodied in the statement 'all is permitted', far from dignifying man, allows him instead to exercise his dark and criminal instincts without fear of divine retribution. In considering Smerdyakov as a parody of Ivan it is to be noted that the onset of mock mental illness in the lackey parallels that of the real thing in Ivan. What is more, several of Smerdyakov's crude aspirations to intellectualism and free-thinking are clearly deformations of stages in Ivan's own intellectual revolt. Thus the latter's insistence upon knowing the details of divine reason is comically echoed in Smerdyakov's question: 'If God created the world on the first day and the sun, moon and stars on the fourth, then where did the light come from on the first day?' (Book III, Ch. 6). A further parody of Ivan's voice, as well as of Cain's reply to God, may be heard in Smerdyakov's insistence that he is not Dmitry's keeper (Book V, Ch. 2). Finally, in what is surely a significant coincidence, Smerdyakov's suicide occurs at the very moment when Ivan is visited by another travesty of his ideas, his hallucinatory devil.

The figure of Dmitry also may be discerned behind Smerdyakov's outline, albeit again in a grotesquely parodistic form. Indeed, the very existence of Smerdyakov as a brother is an affront to the poetry-loving, physically vigorous Dmitry. The sensuous and lyrical confessions of Dmitry to Alyosha (Book III, Chs. 3–5), in which he recounts his passionate love of live, of Grushenka and of Schiller, are followed and travestied by the scene in which the asexual, life-denying, eunuchlike Smerdyakov ironically and passionlessly serenades his neighbour, Mariya Kondratyevna. Dmitry's startling and uninhibited reading of extracts from Schiller is lifelessly echoed in Smerdyakov's high-pitched warbling of a trivial popular song, and monstrously inverted in the lackey's insistence that he dislikes all poetry (Book V, Ch. 2). The symbolic links between Dmitry and Smerdyakov are established again when Dmitry scales the wall of his father's house, assaults Grigory and thus opens the way for Smerdyakov to murder Fyodor Pavlovich. The complicity thus established between the two half-brothers is anticipated in Dmitry's sudden awareness that he has climbed his father's wall at exactly the same spot where years earlier the idiot girl, Liza Smerdyashchaya, came to give birth to Smerdyakov.

There are tenuous but revealing links too between Smerdyakov and Alyosha, the brother who apparently least resembles him. Their mothers, for instance, were both saintly fools, and both were seduced by Fyodor Pavlovich. Alyosha's association with the monastery and the Orthodox faith is parodied in Smerdyakov's apparent association with an extremist sect of religious schismatics, the Castrates, who are the source of certain unsettling motifs in many of Dostoyevsky's works (Peace, *Dostoyevsky: An Examination*). But the most suggestive correspondence is provided in the chapter, 'The Controversy', when Smerdyakov declares that if he ever fell into the hands of heathens he would renounce his Christian faith if by so doing he could save his life. He explains, in terms which the reader will recall during Alyosha's later crisis, how if God refuses to answer his plea for a mountain to move and crush his tormentors he is perfectly justified in denying God in order to save his skin:

But if at precisely that moment I'd tried all that and deliberately cried out to that mountain to crush my tormentors, and if it hadn't crushed them, then tell me, how could I not have doubted at such a dreadful hour of great and mortal terror? Knowing, moreover, that I should never fully attain the Kingdom of Heaven (for if the mountain didn't move at my word, it must mean that they didn't think much of my faith up there and that I wouldn't be in line for much of a reward in the next world), why therefore should I give them my skin to flay and to no good purpose?   (Book III, Ch. 7)

This passage, like Fyodor Pavlovich's comments on hell and its hooks, works on both serious and comic levels. Beneath the nonsense of Smerdyakov's absurd and pretentious intellectual posturing we discern the outline of the spiritual crisis that will later afflict Alyosha. The servant's remarks about abandoning his faith in the absence of a miracle are made ridiculous by the nature of the miracle expected and the juxtaposition of high eloquence ('dreadful hour of great and mortal terror') and crude banality ('I wouldn't be in line for much of a reward...'); but they embody the same reasoning that leads Alyosha to lose his faith. The absence of a miracle on Zosima's death drives the novice to conclude that his own faith has not been rewarded or appreciated, and he temporarily renounces it (Book VII, Ch. 1).

Smerdyakov thus strikes chords in the hearts of all three brothers, and it is clear from the foregoing that, apart from committing the murder, he plays a further important role in the conception of the novel, disclosing the illegitimacy of the Karamazov family by implicating its members in the highly symbolic act of parricide. He achieves this in a variety of ways: by standing as an indictment of the father's moral failure, by exploring and articulating the potential for parricide in the sons, and by travestying and deforming their 'word', that is, all that they stand for, say and do. In his performance of these complex functions Smerdyakov occupies a zone of ambiguity in the novel. Part-person and part-parody, part-human and part-spectre, part-servant and part-master, he is both a son and not a son to Fyodor Pavlovich, and both a brother and not a brother to the sons. Fittingly, in his behaviour and speech, too, he is a master of evasiveness and ambiguity, and nowhere is this more apparent than in his dialogues with Ivan in Books V and XI. The effects of Smerdyakov's speech are cumulative, and they do not emerge in full from a single example, particularly in English translation where the verbal mannerisms are largely lost. The following extracts from his conversation with Ivan, over whether the latter should leave his father to his fate by taking off to Chermashnya, contain characteristically ambiguous pauses, suggestive gestures and implied double meaning:

'He's still asleep, sir [the father],' Smerdyakov pronounced in an unhurried way. ('You were the first to speak, not I,' he seemed to say.) 'I'm surprised at you, sir,' he added after a pause, lowering his eyes in an affected sort of way, putting his right foot forward and playing with the toe of his patent-leather boot ... 'Why, sir, don't you go to Chermashnya, sir?' Smerdyakov said suddenly, looking up and smiling familiarly. ('And you ought to understand yourself why I'm smiling, if you're an intelligent man,' his screwed-up left eye somehow seemed to be saying.)
'Why should I go to Chermashnya?' Ivan asked in surprise. Smerdyakov was silent again.
'Why, Fyodor Pavlovich himself begged you to, sir,' he pronounced at last, unhurriedly and as though not thinking much himself of his reply. ('I'm fobbing you off, as it were, with a third-rate reason, just for something to say,' he appeared to be saying.)
(Book V, Ch. 6)

In Russian the constant repetition of the word *sudar'* (sir) and its common shortened form, the hissing sibilant '-s' added to the end of the preceding word, suggests an improper conspiracy behind the forms of respect, and the particles and ambiguous 'sort ofs', 'somehows', 'as thoughs' and 'as it weres' that litter Smerdyakov's speech serve to enhance its suggestiveness.

This kind of slipperiness provokes Ivan to despair, and his speech to the servant is peppered with phrases like 'Damn

you, man, speak more clearly!', 'I'm afraid I don't understand you', and 'Don't beat about the bush!' The fact is that
Smerdyakov deliberately creates what Morson calls 'verbal
pollution'. He manipulates and abuses language in order to
create anomaly and to destroy the word ('Verbal pollution').
This allows him to generate absurdity, paradox and ambiguity,
and thus to assume the primary function of a travesty: he
destabilises and discredits the ideas represented in the three
brothers by extending their implications into a form not originally intended — that of parricide.

The quest for harmony

The spiritual isolation, psychological fragmentation, and
family disorder of the Karamazovs are often attributed by
them to their fatal 'Karamazov nature'. This takes the form,
variously, of a capacity for chaos, a hedonistic and destructive
sensualism, and a profound but formless rage for life. All
members of the family are affected by this Karamazov nature:
Fyodor Pavlovich in his indiscriminate licentiousness and
aggressive sexuality — he cannot imagine an unattractive
woman; Dmitry in his sense of degradation and his apparently
shameless debauchery; Ivan in his determination to drain
the 'cup of life', no matter how much disgust this costs him.
Even the relatively innocent Alyosha acknowledges the worm
of sensualism deep in his own nature, and it leads him, in
conversation with Liza (or Lise), his 'betrothed', to question
his faith in God:

What we have here is 'the earthy Karamazov force', as Father
Paisy called it the other day, earthy, violent and crude. Whether
the spirit of God moves over this force I do not know. I only know
that I too am a Karamazov. I a monk. A monk? Am I a monk,
Lise? ... It may even be that I do not believe in God.

(Book V, Ch. 1)

But if the 'earthy Karamazov force' leads the brothers to
the horror of parricide and indeed allows them to project the
dark, formless travesty of Smerdyakov to execute this horror,
it nonetheless accounts only for part of their nature. A deeply

significant dualism informs both the perceptions and ultimately the actions of the brothers Karamazov: alongside awareness of their chaotic Karamazov natures all three brothers also possess a developed sense of form, a capacity for aesthetic rapture, a craving for harmony which eludes them in all but their occasional moments of aesthetic insight, but which makes them aware of the inadequacy of their existence and the beastly, fractured, inharmonious nature of man himself. That man is subject to such higher and lower modes of being is a central idea in all of Dostoyevsky's mature fiction. In *Crime and Punishment* Raskolnikov's rationalism, when exercised in isolation from his other faculties, leads him into the impasse of utilitarian morality, which justifies the act of violence and allows the murder of a fellow human being if it yields socially desirable consequences. But his crime, condoned by reason, is censured by what Dostoyevsky described as 'unsuspected and unanticipated feelings' which 'torment his heart' (rather than his head) and compel him to give himself up. These feelings derive from a higher mode of being than the rational. They are the product of Raskolnikov's aesthetic sense, which discloses to the murderer the ugliness of the act of violence. The point is that in Dostoyevsky's aesthetic system the moral and aesthetic categories are indissolubly linked and one can act as an indicator of the other. R.L. Jackson has shown how Dostoyevsky's aesthetic views centred on the concept of ideal beauty which migrated from Plato, through medieval Christian aesthetics, to Schiller, Schelling and Hegel (*Dostoevsky's Quest for Form*). It was no doubt from his lifelong interest in the work of Schiller that Dostoyevsky derived his belief in the possibility of the moral transfiguration of man through his aesthetic awareness. To his friend Strakhov he remarked: 'only that is moral which coincides with your feeling of beauty', an idea which Dostoyevsky's favourite hero, Prince Myshkin, develops when he asserts that 'beauty will save the world'. Man's innate receptiveness to ideal beauty − a receptiveness lost only in the most hopelessly fallen human soul − is for Dostoyevsky the clearest evidence of his participation in some higher, absolute, unifying, harmonious order, which lies beyond

his rational awareness, and which promises ultimate reconciliation of his discords and moral despair in the chaos of
earthly existence. As we shall see, all three of the Karamazov
brothers are drawn to this higher harmony even though they
cannot understand or accommodate it within their normal
mode of being. Their craving for harmony cannot be satisfied
by the logic of Ivan, the sensual experiments of Dmitry, or
Alyosha's conventional veneer of faith. None of them can find
a temporal equivalent or embodiment of the higher order they
sense: in Ivan's experience the mathematical harmonies of
rational analysis expire in a cul-de-sac where he is confronted
with their inadequacy; to Dmitry the inharmonious, primitive
formlessness of his physical urges brings despair; and the
frail tranquillity of Alyosha's monastic retreat fails to with-
stand the encroachment of worldly disorder. This last point
is anticipated at the very start of the novel when the divided
Karamazov family invades the reflective peace of the monastic
cell. Subsequently the introduction of Father Ferapont and
his opposition to Zosima eloquently conveys the petty discords
and squabbling hidden within the monastery itself. Zosima
recognises the frailty of monastic harmony when he sends
Alyosha out into the world. The young novice must experience
moral chaos, he must face up to his 'Karamazov nature'
instead of concealing it beneath a cassock, before he can find
a lasting harmony.

The dualism explored in *The Brothers Karamazov* between
the earthly, chaotic Karamazov force and an enduring sense
of a higher harmonious existence serves to recapitulate two
major, and apparently contradictory, strands of Dostoyevsky's
earlier work: his belief in the inadequacy of all man's attempts
to create a harmonious world order on secular foundations,
and his lifelong preoccupation with the ideal of the Golden
Age. For Dostoyevsky man's aspirations to a harmonious
earthly existence were inevitably blocked by the fact that 'we
do not have a nature capable of brotherhood', and any political,
moral or intellectual system which sought salvation in the
secular world without first addressing the religious question
of man's fallen and degraded state was doomed to failure.

Yet even in his despair man could be rescued from his bestiality through his abiding memory of a lost paradise, his longing for a Golden Age of primal harmony and innocence. The fact that such a longing has to remain a dream while man's nature goes unredeemed by religious transfiguration is clarified by the failure of the 'positively good man', Prince Myshkin in *The Idiot*, to translate his luminous ideals into earthly harmony and by the warning he receives that 'Paradise on earth is not easily achieved ... Paradise is a difficult thing, Prince, much more difficult than it seems to your good heart' (VIII, 282). A similar lesson that paradise is not to be secured through naive utopianism is learned by Alyosha Karamazov when he seeks to make amends for Dmitry's insult to the Snegiryov family by offering money to allow little Ilyusha to be taken to a warmer province. For a moment he and Snegiryov are drawn into utopian complicity − 'We shall always be brothers ... No, it is not a dream!' he cries rapturously − before Snegiryov's pride compels him to reject the offer and throw the money to the ground (Book IV, Ch. 7).

The idea that the dream of a Golden Age represents a glimpse of a higher harmony which is not translatable into temporal forms is clarified by Dostoyevsky's use of geometric metaphor in *The Brothers Karamazov*. He appears to challenge Voltaire's assertion in the *Dictionnaire Philosophique* that 'there is but one morality, as there is but one geometry', when he has Ivan refer to the limitations of Euclidean reason. Dostoyevsky implies a contrast between the 'higher logic' of the modern non-Euclidean geometries and classical Euclidean geometry, and he uses the analogy of non-Euclidean geometry in order to suggest the existence of another world and of a higher order beyond that accessible to man's rational under-standing. But he derives his immediate inspiration for this idea from quite another source: his friendship with the out-standing young mystic and philosopher, Vladimir Sergeyevich Solovyov (1853−1900), who accompanied the distraught Dostoyevsky to Optina Pustyn after the death of his son. The two were therefore particularly close during the period when Dostoyevsky was at work on *The Brothers Karamazov*.

It is widely acknowledged that Alyosha Karamazov was partly modelled on Solovyov, and it is also likely that some of the latter's intellectual characteristics (he had undergone an atheistic phase in the 1860s) were incorporated in the portrait of Ivan.

In Solovyov's philosophy the natural world, the world of man, had fallen away from divine unity and as a result appeared discordant and chaotic, but behind this apparent disintegration the original ideal unity was preserved as potential. The point of contact between these coexisting natural and ideal worlds was man himself, since he belonged to both spheres and was both 'deity and nothingness':

Since our natural world is also and necessarily connected in the closest way to this divine world ... and since there is not and cannot be any impassable gulf between them, individual rays and glimmerings of the divine world must penetrate into our actual world, constituting the ideal content, the beauty and truth, which we find in it. Man, as a member of both worlds, can and must establish contact with the divine world by an act of intellectual intuition (*umstvennoye sozertsaniye*). While remaining in the world of struggle and dark anxiety, he can and must enter into communion with the clear forms of the realm of glory and eternal beauty.

(*Russian Philosophy*, Vol. III, p. 73)

Dostoyevsky no doubt found in these words a clear confirmation of his own sense of man's simultaneous experience of higher and lower modes of being, as his existence in the discordant and fortuitous world of nature is relieved by the premonition of a Golden Age. The dualism described by Solovyov is clearly built into Dostoyevsky's conception of the Karamazov sons. Each of them experiences in the course of the novel moments of mystical insight, of 'non-Euclidean' harmony which is both compelling and liberating. It liberates in so far as it promotes in the brothers an awareness of participation in some higher harmonious whole and offers them refuge from their base, fragmented, chaotic and limited Karamazov natures.

It is possible that Dostoyevsky also drew upon Solovyov's thought in his conception of the three brothers as schematic representations of the three kinds of human knowledge: physical experience (Dmitry), intellectual reason (Ivan) and intuitive faith (Alyosha). Solovyov too identified these three forms of knowledge, and argued that the first two are made meaningful only by the last. Faith provides a content for abstract reason and a form for experience: without the faith of Alyosha, Dmitry's physical experience remains a chaotic quest for form and Ivan's reason becomes an empty exercise in formal logic.

It is perhaps Dmitry who embodies most clearly the conflict between higher and lower modes of being. He is conscious of some intangible harmony — something perhaps like Pascal's *agrément* — in which the whole of creation apart from man, and especially apart from Dmitry himself, appears to participate. Dmitry regards himself as a beast, as an 'insect with lust', and he is ashamed of his body, his physical excesses, and his chaotic lack of self-control. These, he feels, debase the ecstatic harmony he sometimes senses, a harmony which stands in such tormenting contrast to the physical and moral squalor with which he surrounds himself. Dmitry's sense of aesthetic alienation is, in some respects at least, comparable to that of Myshkin, who through a physical clumsiness occasioned by illness feels unable to participate in the harmonious chorus of God's world. The fact that Myshkin senses this harmony but fears that he might debase it makes his estrangement from it all the more poignant.

The existence of some higher purpose, of some cosmic consonance, behind the ugliness of earthly existence is revealed to Dmitry, as it is to his brothers, in moments of aesthetic rapture. For Dmitry, the brother most identified with physicality, this rapture accompanies a primitive pagan exultation in the physical joys of life. A profoundly sensual person, he is easy prey to drink, emotional excess and the seductive curves of his beloved Grushenka. His very name points to his pagan nature: Demeter was the Greek goddess of the earth and agriculture, and Dmitry is a true child of the earth. In moments of intense exultation Dmitry's thirst for harmony is temporarily slaked by poetry, an evocative and appropriate metaphor for the sense of life contained within a harmonious form. But even in his choice of poetry Dmitry confirms his pagan nature: he cites Schiller's 'Eleusinian Festival', followed by his 'Ode to Joy' with its clearly pagan delight in nature and life:

> Joy eternal gives drink
> To the soul of God's creation,
> And enflames the cup of life
> With the secret force of fermentation.
> It has drawn the grass to the light,
> Has developed chaos into suns
> And scattered them out in the voids
> Beyond the astrologer's ken.
> At the bosom of bounteous nature
> All that breathes drinks of joy;
> All creatures, all nations
> Are drawn after her.
> In misfortune she has given us friends:
> The juice of grapes, the garlands of the graces;
> To the insects she has given sensualism ...
> The Angel faces God.   (Book III, Ch. 3)

But Dmitry's primitive pagan receptivity to the joy of being, his intoxication with life, is not controlled by a moral form. As he confesses to Alyosha, he finds that the 'cup of life' spills over equally easily into debauchery or adoration, into sensuality or spiritual ecstasy. The breadth and all-consuming nature of his appetite for life oppress Dmitry as a mystery: 'There's an awful lot of mysteries! Too many enigmas oppress man on earth ... Yes, man is too broad, too broad indeed! I would narrow him down ...' (Book III, Ch. 3). The crown of this mystery is beauty, which for Dmitry seems to possess a dreadful ambiguity. The breadth of his aesthetic instincts allows him to detect what he regards as beauty in both vice and virtue, in Sodom as well as in the Madonna, and he is susceptible to both types:

Beauty is a fearful and terrifying thing! Terrible because it's indefinable, and it's impossible to define because God presents nothing but enigmas. Here the shores meet, here all contradictions live together ... Beauty! Besides, I cannot bear it that a man, even though noble of soul and with a fine mind, should start from the ideal of the Madonna and end with the ideal of Sodom. It's even more terrible when a man with the ideal of Sodom already in his heart does not renounce the ideal of the Madonna ... What appears to the mind as shameful is sheer beauty to the heart. Is there beauty in Sodom? Believe me, for the vast majority of people it is indeed in Sodom – did you not know that? It is terrifying that beauty is not only a terrible, but also a mysterious thing. Here God and the Devil struggle for mastery, and the battlefield is the heart of man.

(Book III, Ch. 3)

Dmitry's sense of the ambiguity of beauty, so central to this novel of disorder, clearly shows Dostoyevsky's awareness of Solovyov's view of man as a vehicle mediating between the natural and ideal worlds, susceptible equally to the chaos and evil of the earth and the divine beauty of heaven. The philosopher's abstractions are fleshed out by the novelist; they are endured by Dmitry as a moral dilemma and articulated in the only way he knows − in formless, poetic ecstasy:

If I am to fly into the abyss [of debauchery], then I shall do so precipitously, headlong, and shall even be pleased to find myself in such a degrading situation, shall consider it beautiful as far as I'm concerned. But in the very depths of that shame I shall suddenly begin a hymn. Let me be cursed, let me be low and base, but let me also kiss the hem of that garment in which my God is cloaked; even if I'm chasing after the Devil at that very moment, I am still your son, O Lord, and I love you, and I feel that joy without which the world could not be ... (Book III, Ch. 3)

Dmitry's sensitivity to 'the beauty of the Madonna' clearly derives from Dostoyevsky's conviction that the need for ideal beauty is as natural to man as eating or breathing, an idea which he elaborated as early as 1861 in his essay 'Mr —bov and the Question of Art' and which is central to his aesthetic system. Man, oppressed by the limitations, distractions and formlessness of his physical existence, craves an absolute harmony, a fusion of his moral and aesthetic ideals, which stimulates him to moral progress and in which he can seek release, redemption and eventual reconciliation. On the other hand, the idea of finding an 'aesthetic' appeal in the Sodom of deliberate self-abasement and the wilful perversion of one's higher instincts Dmitry inherits from his father, and indeed from a whole gallery of rebellious Dostoyevskian characters, beginning with Golyadkin (*The Double*) and the hero of 'Polzunkov' in the 1840s, and culminating in the Underground Man and the civil servant Marmeladov from *Crime and Punishment*. Early in *The Brothers Karamazov* Fyodor Pavlovich confesses to Zosima that he abases himself largely to gratify his aesthetic feelings: 'Exactly! Exactly! I've been debasing myself all my life for pleasure, for the sake of my aesthetic feelings, for it's not only pleasant, but sometimes even beautiful to be offended!' (Book II, Ch. 2). This perverse sense of beauty in Sodom had already been dismissed by Dostoyevsky in 'Mr —bov and the Question of Art' as an aesthetic aberration and a symptom of moral decline:

We have seen examples where man, having achieved the ideal of his desires and not knowing what else to aim for, being totally satiated, has fallen into a kind of anguish, has even exacerbated this anguish within himself, has sought out another ideal in life and out of extreme surfeit has not only ceased to value that which he enjoys, but has even consciously turned away from the straight path and has fomented in himself strange, unhealthy, sharp, inharmonious, sometimes even monstrous tastes, losing measure and aesthetic feeling for healthy beauty and demanding instead of it exceptions.   (XVIII, 94)

Fyodor Pavlovich is just such a lost soul, and he sees ideal beauty as merely a spice to enliven his taste for the beauty of Sodom, and vice versa. This explains his perverse, asexual attraction to the saintly mother of Ivan and Alyosha as a foil to his sensualist nature. Dmitry, though, is far less capable of accepting his disturbingly divided aesthetic appetite. His moments of harmonious release do not allow him to live easily with his own moral chaos, and his quest for a definite moral form to contain his physical vigour is clearly revealed by his actions throughout the novel. He describes in desperate terms the degraded state of mankind in general by quoting Schiller's account of the horrors which confront Ceres − significantly, the Roman equivalent of Demeter, Dmitry's namesake − when she descends to earth from the Olympian heights:

> The fruit of the fields and the sweet grapes
> Do not gleam at the feasts;
> Only the remains of corpses
> Smoke on the bloody altars;
> And wherever Ceres casts
> Her melancholy gaze
> She sees man everywhere
> Sunk in deepest degradation!   (Book III, Ch. 3)

Dmitry also confesses his preoccupation with the degradation of man's earthly life in more personal terms and goes
on, in a conversation with Perkhotin, the young civil servant
to whom he pawns his pistols, to couch his craving for form
and harmony in less oblique language. The conversation
occurs after one of Dmitry's monumental orgies:

'You know, my friend,' Dmitry said suddenly with feeling, 'I've
never liked all this disorder.'
'Who does! Fancy wasting three dozen bottles on peasants. That
would make anyone's blood boil.'
'No, I don't mean that. I'm speaking of a higher order. I have
no order in me, no higher order ... The whole of my life has been
disorder, and I must impose order ...
    Glory to the highest on earth,
    Glory to the highest in me!
That verse once burst from my soul; it's not a verse, but a tear ...'
                                                    (Book VIII, Ch. 5)

The humour of the misunderstanding in this conversation
is a perfect counterpoint to Dmitry's despair: his recognition
of the existence of 'the highest in him' − further evidence
perhaps of Solovyov's influence in this part of the novel
− is confounded by the disgust he feels at his Karamazov
nature. He is thus prepared to destroy himself for the sake
of a higher harmony, for he feels that his own existence is
an intolerable stain upon that divine order. He obtains the
opportunity for such a sacrifice when he is arrested for the
murder of his father, but he does not acquire the moral awareness, or faith, needed to direct his sense of life until after
his arrest. He dreams during his interrogation of the apparently
needless sufferings of a starving child, and the barriers of
self-absorption and isolation are breached by a growing sense
of responsibility for the misfortune of others, in particular
the child:

And he felt that his heart was touched in a way it had never been
touched before, that he wanted to cry, that he wished to do something in order that neither the baby nor its black, shrivelled mother
would ever have to cry again, so that there would be no further
need for anyone's tears from that moment on.   (Book IX, Ch. 8)

This moment marks the start of Dmitry's transfiguration, as he prepares to take the sufferings of others upon himself. He is prepared to go to Siberia, not for the particular crime of parricide with which he is charged, but for the crimes of humanity as a whole, distilled in the image of the suffering child, an image designed, no doubt, to recall the misery of Ilyusha Snegiryov. Dmitry's dream is a revelation which transforms his sense of life from self-centred, directionless, pagan ecstasy to a Christian religious and moral passion. He is transformed by the novel's central doctrine that 'all are responsible', his Karamazov nature is vanquished, and his isolation from the rest of creation is at an end. 'I've felt the presence of a new man in me − a new man has arisen in me!' he cries to Alyosha. 'He was locked within me, but he would never have appeared had it not been for this thunderbolt' (Book XI, Ch. 4). At this moment, as he takes on the sins of humanity and embarks upon the road to Calvary, Dmitry assumes the appearance of Christ, and the new man that has arisen in him is the *God-man* envisaged by Solovyov, whose role is to restore the world of man to the world of God.

Ivan Karamazov, too, experiences moments of release and self-sublimation, moments when his chronic self-awareness and intellectual autonomy dissolve in a sense of the harmonious fusion of all God's creation. As with Dmitry, Ivan's craving for harmony originates in an awareness of the ugliness and disorder of human life and of the presence of the 'Karamazov force' in his soul. He cites Voltaire's well-known remark about the existence of God, 's'il n'existait pas Dieu il faudrait l'inventer', and then suggests that man's need for God satisfies a craving for a higher harmony which dignifies him even in his squalor:

But what is so strange and marvellous is not that God actually exists, but that such a thought − the idea of the necessity of God − should have crept into the head of so savage and wicked a creature as man; so holy is it, so touching and so wise, and so much does it redound to man's honour.
                                                                    (Book V, Ch. 3)

Such a redeeming need for divine harmony is present in Ivan himself. Surprisingly, perhaps, he confesses to Alyosha something that clearly aligns him with Dmitry: his passionate, irrational and undisciplined thirst for life. He even describes this thirst in the very image used by Dmitry: Schiller's 'cup of life', which Ivan cannot renounce until he has drained it. Ivan's knowledge of Schiller, which surprises Alyosha, is used by Dostoyevsky as a form of shorthand to suggest the intellectual brother's sense of life and capacity for aesthetic response, which is later confirmed in Ivan's admission that he suffers a duality of perception similar to Dmitry's. He is instinctively drawn to the beauty of God's world, as condensed in the image of the 'sticky, little leaves in spring', but this contradicts his intellectual disgust at the way God has ordered creation. In other words, Ivan's intellectual arrogance and independence are shaken by an instinct for a higher order that is beyond his rational comprehension: 'This isn't intellect; it isn't logic; it's something you love with your insides, from your belly... I want to live, and I shall live, albeit in spite of logic ... Even if I've lost faith in the order of things; even if I'm convinced that, on the contrary, everything is disordered, damned and perhaps even chaos created by the Devil ... I nonetheless wish to live' (Book V, Ch. 3).

But perhaps Ivan transcends the limits of his purely intellectual knowledge most radically in his *rapturous* anticipation of God's final harmonious reconciliation, when all chaos and anguish will be dispersed in the grace that will fill the universe: 'And so I accept God; and not only willingly, but what is more I accept also His infinite wisdom and His purpose, which we are not given to understand. I believe in the order and meaning of life, I believe in the eternal harmony into which we are all supposed to flow, I believe in the Word towards which the universe is striving and which was "with God and is God", and so on ...' (Book V, Ch. 3). The dry 'and so on ...' here reminds us that by the end of this passage Dostoyevsky has allowed the sceptic in Ivan to reassert himself. But the novelist has nonetheless had his hero speak with genuine, if reluctant, ardour of a state of universal consonance, similar to that envisaged in Solovyov's teachings, where the will of man merges with that of God and the gulf between the natural and divine worlds is bridged. The irony is that, although Ivan senses the inevitability of this reconciliation, he is compelled to reject it for two very important reasons, which indicate his contrary impulse to pit his will against the divine order in an impressive act of metaphysical rebellion. First, the existence of this higher, supra-rational harmony is, for Ivan, an affront to the dignity and independence of rational man, whose understanding is confined to the three dimensions of Euclidean logic. In this respect Dostoyevsky presents Ivan as an archetypal victim of Original Sin: tormented by the memory of Eden in his moments of aesthetic insight, he cannot accommodate these experiences within the framework of strict, analytical logic. Created by Dostoyevsky to be a modern man, proud of his reason and enlightenment, Ivan is unable to deny the supremacy of his logical perception in favour of some intangible, indefinable sense of spiritual well-being. Surely, he argues, if God had wished us to participate in His mystical purpose He should have allowed us to understand His 'mysterious ways' by endowing us with minds capable of transcending the purely logical. Ivan construes God's apparent refusal to do so not as the gift of freedom of faith to man, but as a slight upon that crown of all human endeavour – rational analysis. Ivan, a nineteenth-century European intellectual, is compelled to pledge his allegiance to logic rather than to intuition, to place 'the understanding of life' (*soznaniye zhizni*) higher than 'the sense of life' (*chuvstvo zhizni*). The understanding of life dignifies man; the mere sense of it debases him by reducing him to the status of the animals. Perhaps this accounts above all else for Ivan's intense dislike of his brother Dmitry, whose behaviour wantonly proclaims a base sense of life and an absence of all analytical understanding. Ivan's unwillingness to accept the love of life as more important than understanding its meaning distinguishes him also from Alyosha, who urges him to 'love life regardless of logic, as you say; yes, most certainly regardless of logic, for only then will you grasp its meaning' (Book V, Ch. 3). Dostoyevsky neatly exposes their different attitudes by implicitly comparing Ivan's comments about Europe being a graveyard with Alyosha's behaviour after his rebirth of faith

(Book VII, Ch. 4). In his moment of sublime insight, Alyosha falls to the ground and drenches it with his tears. This for him is a moment of ecstasy, when his love of creation overcomes his inability to understand God's apparent refusal to crown the life of the deceased Zosima with a miracle. Previously Ivan, too, has spoken of drenching the earth with his tears, but the earth he had in mind was that heaped upon the graves of his beloved European rationalist philosophers, those 'understanders' of life, the champions of scepticism rather than faith.

Moreover, Ivan's Euclidean mind cannot accept a harmony that can accommodate, without apparently *correcting*, the brutal moral discords introduced into this world by mankind's cruelty and inhumanity. Significantly in the context of Dmitry's conversion through the image of a suffering child, Ivan illustrates his hatred of moral ugliness and justifies his rebellion by reference to the torture of children. The tears of these innocent victims of perverse inhumanity must, he demands, be avenged and all injustice resolved; but Ivan's concrete, rectilinear mind can be appeased only by concrete, rectilinear justice, in this world rather than in the next. God's higher harmony, the inevitability of which Ivan is prepared to concede, is *improper* because man's brutish behaviour spoils it. Ivan is therefore forced to the conclusion that temporal chaos must be countered not by God's redeeming non-Euclidean grace, but by an imposed temporal order, represented most vividly in his unwritten poem 'The Grand Inquisitor', but already implicit in an earlier article he has written on the relations between Church and State. The full implications of Ivan's 'poem' and article must be examined later.

As he did with Dmitry, Dostoyevsky provides the key to Ivan's eventual 'conversion' in the form of a dream, a product of Ivan's subconscious and his aesthetic sense, rather than of his rational mind. Dmitry's dream of the baby offers him a form in which to express his sense of life and, along with his willingness to accept suffering, it completes his moral regeneration. Ivan's rebirth is not, however, completed within the novel; it is only begun. Dmitry's failing was a lack of form; Ivan's is a lack of content. He is fully armed with the 'form' of rational analysis which he tries to impose upon the stuff of life. But that same rational analysis strips life of meaningful content, forces him consciously to reject its joys, and confronts him with the abyss of negation and non-being. Ivan's conversion can begin only when the 'forms' of reason are undermined by that same instinct which draws him to the 'sticky, little leaves in spring'. Dostoyevsky achieves this in several ways. First, Ivan's rational assertion of the moral independence of man and the doctrine of 'all is permitted' are stripped of all form and grandeur when they are travestied in the behaviour of Smerdyakov. Secondly, Ivan's constant disgust when confronted with the ugliness of the lackey and his behaviour is presented as an indication that his aesthetic sense is repelled by the incarnation of ideas that are acceptable to his reason. Thirdly, and most important, the crown of Ivan's rational revolt, 'The Grand Inquisitor', is thoroughly undermined by another travesty, that offered in Ivan's fevered nightmare when he is visited by the Devil on the eve of Dmitry's trial (Book XI, Ch. 9).

The Devil, who has been troubling Ivan's imagination for some time and who finally confronts him after his critical interviews with Smerdyakov (when Ivan learns the truth about his father's murder), is a *reductio ad absurdum* of Ivan's earlier intellectual positions, of his proud rational rebellion against divine order, and of his greatest creation, that ultimate embodiment of rational humanism, the Grand Inquisitor. In the course of his nightmare Ivan is compelled to recognise all this: 'Everything that is stupid in my nature, everything that I've already lived through and hammered out in my mind long ago, everything I've thrown aside like so much carrion − all this you present to me like something new!' (Book XI, Ch. 9). But what strikes Ivan as different here is not the content of the Devil's ideas, but their distasteful form, and this is why he tries to distance himself by calling his alter-ego 'you'. The embodiment of Ivan's ideas in the majestic figure of the Inquisitor was the product of intellect alone − he confesses to Alyosha that he thought up this 'poem' but has not been able to write it down and thus give it form. The Devil, however, is the product of Ivan's aesthetic sense at a moment when his reason fails and starts to disintegrate. As a result this incarnation of Ivan's revolt is distinctly shabby and unappealing, a rheumatic demon in threadbare clothes and with a head cold. 'How could my soul have begotten a lackey such as you?' Ivan cries as he struggles to reconcile the grandeur of his intellectual designs with the absurdity of their present embodiment. Yet his final interview with Smerdyakov, which immediately preceded this nightmare, must serve to remind Ivan that the present Devil is not the only obscene 'lackey' begotten by his rebellious intellect.

The Devil himself recognises Ivan's confusion — hardly surprisingly, since he is a product of Ivan's own delirium: 'I see that you positively expect something great and perhaps something beautiful from me. That's a great shame, for I only give what I can'. He then continues:

I repeat, moderate your demands. Don't demand from me 'everything great and beautiful' and you'll see how well we'll get on together... In truth, you are annoyed at me because I did not appear to you in some sort of red glow, 'with thunder and lightning' and with scorched wings, but introduced myself in so modest a guise. You are offended first in your aesthetic feelings and then in your pride. How, you wonder, could such a vulgar devil appear to such a great man? No, I'm afraid you have that romantic strain so derided by Belinsky.

(Book XI, Ch. 9)

This passage, like much of the rest of the nightmare, is rich in parody of Ivan's deepest beliefs, and enlivened by sarcastic references to youthful idealism and that icon of Russian progressive thought, Belinsky. In this way Ivan exposes his own intellectual posturing and betrays the frailty of his convictions. A more detailed analysis of the relationship of the Devil's 'voice' to that of Ivan must, however, be left until later in this study.

Alyosha too is rescued from revolt by a dream, or vision, which discloses the existence of a higher, all-embracing, all-redeeming order beyond the chaos of earthly life. Although Alyosha's role in the novel is to represent faith, the faith he possesses is naive, untried, precarious and susceptible to challenge from both his Karamazov sensualism and his rational doubts. This faith is tested when confronted with the combination of Zosima's death and unseemly putrefaction, and the full force of Ivan's rejection of God. Momentarily Alyosha falls into despair, his faith falters, and he consciously draws upon Ivan's words when he remarks to Rakitin: 'I am not rebelling against my God, I simply "don't accept his world"' (Book VII, Ch. 2). He feels that justice has been violated by the undignified end to the life of his mentor: 'It was justice, justice that [Alyosha] thirsted for, and not just miracles! And now the man who, according to his hopes, ought to have been raised above all others in the world, that very man, instead of receiving the glory due to him, was suddenly cast down and disgraced! What for? Who had so judged? Who could decide thus?' (Book VII, Ch. 2). This is indeed 'open rebellion', but, unlike Ivan, Alyosha does not allow his intellectual doubts to disqualify his instinctive sense of the higher justice and order of creation. The miracle missing from Zosima's death is eventually presented by Dostoyevsky in the 'non-Euclidean' form of Father Paisy's reading of the biblical account of the wedding at Cana of Galilee, when Christ turned water into wine and proclaimed the joy of existence. Alyosha's frame of mind during this reading — part-prayer and part-trance — prepares his soul for the revelation of Zosima's immortality and the mystical union of heaven and earth:

His soul, filled with rapture, craved freedom, room, space. The dome of heaven was inverted above his head, vast, boundless, and studded with silent, shining stars. The Milky Way, still elusive, ran from zenith to horizon in two arms. The night, fresh, silent and still, enfolded the earth. The white towers and golden domes of the church gleamed against the sapphire sky. The luxuriant spring flowers in the beds around the house fell asleep till morning. The stillness of the earth seemed somehow to merge with that of the heavens. The mystery of the earth came into contact with that of the stars ... Alyosha stood and looked, and suddenly he fell to the ground as if he'd been cut down.

He didn't know why he was embracing it; he was not aware of why he longed so irresistibly to kiss it, to kiss it all, but he kissed it, weeping, sobbing and drenching it with his tears; and he vowed in a frenzy to love it, to love it till the end of time. 'Water the earth with the tears of your joy and love those tears', rang out in his heart. Why was he weeping? Oh, in his rapture he was weeping even over those stars which shone on him from out of the abyss, and 'he was not ashamed of his frenzy'. It was as if threads from all those innumerable worlds of God came together at once in his soul, and it was all a-tremble 'as it touched other worlds'. He wanted to forgive all men for all things and to beg forgiveness − oh, not for himself, but for all men, for everyone and everything. 'And others will plead for me' − this rang out in his soul again. And with each moment he felt clearly and in a way almost tangibly that something firm and immovable, like that heavenly vault, was entering his soul. Some sort of idea was taking possession of his mind − and would rule it for the rest of his life, for all time. He had fallen to the ground a weak youth, but he rose from it a resolute fighter for the rest of his life, and he realised and felt this suddenly at the very moment of his rapture...

(Book VII, Ch. 4)

This vision, completely devoid of the scepticism with which Dostoyevsky invests Ivan's thoughts and possessed of a form and a tranquillity absent from Dmitry's rapture, is the most complete description we have in *The Brothers Karamazov* of the sense of harmony experienced by all three brothers, and as such it is at the centre of the religious design of both this novel and of Dostoyevsky's work as a whole. It is therefore fitting that it should betray, in its references to the contiguous existence of heaven and earth and to the threads unifying the universe, the influence exercised upon Dostoyevsky by the thought of both Solovyov and Fyodorov. From his encounters with the ideas of these thinkers Dostoyevsky distilled a powerful image of divine order to oppose the chaos and fragmentation explored in his novel.

Pro and contra

The dualism of the brothers Karamazov, their suspension between the chaos of their Karamazov natures and the profound sense of a lost harmony which they yearn to recover, allows Dostoyevsky to develop a rich mythical seam in his novel, centred on the biblical story of the Fall of Man. Indeed it was perhaps from Genesis, with its account of the creation of man from both the dust of the earth and the breath of God, that

Dostoyevsky drew his theme of man's potential for both higher and lower modes of being. Moreover, the human weaknesses of the Karamazov sons assume metaphorical significance when it is seen that, as well as being individual failings, they also contain echoes of that first act of 'parricide': Original Sin and the Fall. In the biblical account, man's taste of the forbidden fruit from the tree of knowledge is analogous to Ivan's experience in the novel: it represents the acquisition of intellectual arrogance and the potential for divine rebellion, as Adam and Eve seek to *know for themselves* the nature of good and evil, hitherto the prerogative of God alone. They become as God, just as Ivan demands to know the ways of God, and they place what Ivan would call 'the understanding of life' (*soznaniye zhizni*) higher than the joy of life. The consciousness they thus acquire subsequently alienates them from the rest of creation. The acquisition of knowledge also leads in Genesis to self-consciousness and a sense of bodily shame. When the Lord asks Adam why he has concealed his nakedness behind a figleaf, Adam replies: 'I was afraid, because I was naked' (Genesis 3: 10). This too is clearly echoed in *The Brothers Karamazov* by Dmitry's physical disgust at himself and particularly by his overwhelming sense of shame after his arrest as he stands naked before his prosecutors. Significantly, both Adam and Dmitry display this bodily shame when confronted with the accusation that they have turned against their 'fathers': Adam by having betrayed the trust of the Lord; Dmitry by apparently having killed Fyodor Pavlovich. A further link is established between Adam and Dmitry when we remember that as a punishment for tasting the forbidden fruit Adam is banished from Eden, along with Eve, and told to till the soil. Dmitry and Grushenka also contemplate purging their sins by a life of exile in America, where they intend to work the soil. Dmitry's name, suggesting as it does the goddess of agriculture, adds further weight to this interpretation.

Alyosha too is metaphorically implicated in Original Sin. Adam's decision to eat the fruit of the tree of knowledge must be seen as a failure of faith in God in the face of diabolic temptation. Dostoyevsky has Alyosha yield to a comparable temptation, proffered on this occasion not by Satan but by that other advocate of rebellion against God's order, his brother Ivan. As we have seen, Ivan's arguments conspire with Alyosha's disappointment at the lack of a miracle upon Zosima's death to promote in the young novice a severe, if temporary, crisis of faith, during which the murder of Fyodor Pavlovich takes place.

Such 'intertextuality', the embedding of motifs from Genesis (and, indeed, from other books of the Bible) into the narrative framework of *The Brothers Karamazov*, helps to introduce the novel's main philosophical pivot: the confrontation between earthly and divine concepts of justice and order. The Fall of Man is of central importance to the Christian world-view: it marks the destruction of the harmonious order of world paradise; it signals the moment when God's justice was first subjected to the scrutiny of man, when man claimed the right to oppose his own knowledge of good and evil and his own sense of proper order to the moral order created by God. Indirect references to Original Sin in a novel about the fragmentation of a family, the breakdown of moral order and the turning of sons against father, are thus entirely apt and suggestive: in the tragedy of the Karamazov family the Fall of Man is replayed.

All three Karamazov brothers display a sustained preoccupation with the questions of justice and order. Alyosha, for example, is offended by what he regards as the injustice and moral 'disorder' of Zosima's undignified and inappropriate end; Dmitry simmers with a constant sense of injustice and disorder — at the loss of his inheritance, at the blemish which his own chaotic nature inflicts upon the harmony of creation, and finally at the sufferings of an innocent babe and its mother. But it is Ivan who imparts a theoretical dimension to these questions, thus preparing the way for what Dostoyevsky regarded as the core and 'culminating point' of his novel: the implied conflict between the world of the Grand Inquisitor and that of the Russian monk in Books V and VI.

As Malcolm Jones has observed, Ivan's intellectual stance derives from his having concluded that even if God exists he is not 'the sort of God from whom principles of virtue can be derived', since his creation is unjust and erected upon the sufferings of the innocent (*Dostoyevsky: The Novel of Discord*). This leads Ivan to reject divine justice, and to advocate instead temporal and secular schemes and structures in which his own sense of justice and order can find expression. His views on divine and temporal concepts of justice and order are first articulated, albeit in a strangely ambivalent form, in the discussion in Zosima's cell of an article Ivan has written on the subject of ecclesiastical courts (Book II, Ch. 5). This article is a polemical piece, characteristic of the 1860s when questions of justice and law occupied a prominent place in Russian journalism. The view that Ivan advances in it is not, however, typical of a young radical of that decade. Having described the historical separation of Church and State and the demarcation of their areas of influence into the spiritual and secular spheres respectively, Ivan draws a surprising conclusion. He appears to reject the view that the Church should seek a role in the State 'like any other social organisation', or that its ideals should be either enforced by temporal power, as in the Roman Church, or transmuted into a secular form such as utopian socialism. Such aspirations, he argues, are symptomatic of the paganism which informed the Roman state and which was later transmitted to Catholicism and the whole of Western civilisation. Instead Ivan advances a view more characteristic of Russian Orthodoxy and classical Slavophilism:

On the contrary, every earthly state must eventually be completely transformed into a Church, and become nothing but a Church, even renouncing those of its aims that are incompatible with those of a Church. All this will in no way diminish it or deprive it of its honour and glory as a great state, nor will it detract from the glory of its rulers. It will merely turn it away from a false, mistaken and still pagan path to the right and true path which alone leads to the eternal goals.

(Book II, Ch. 5)

The realisation of this ideal would, Ivan argues, profoundly change the nature of crime, justice and punishment, for the criminal who is now prepared to break man's law and risk man's justice and punishment as represented by the State, would surely baulk at the prospect of transgressing God's law and incurring His punishment, as meted out by the Church:

If everything became the Church, then the Church would excommunicate the criminal and disobedient, and not cut off their heads. Where, I ask you, would the excommunicated go? Why, they would have to renounce the company not only of men, as now, but also of Christ.   (Book II, Ch. 5)

It would appear that Ivan is arguing that both the social order and the justice offered by the spiritual world of the Church should replace the secular equivalents offered by the State. Man's justice and order are inferior to those of God working through His Church — this is the startling and uncharacteristic message of Ivan's exposition. Father Joseph, the librarian, is the first of Ivan's listeners to detect a false note in all this, but his enthusiastic endorsement of Ivan's conclusions diverts him from his instinctive sense that something is wrong. He observes that the idea of Ivan's article 'appears to cut both ways', and of course he is right. Despite Ivan's apparent advocacy of the State-turned-Church, his article inevitably raises the spectre of something quite different: the Church-turned-State. In Ivan's dialectic the Russian Orthodox ideal of a divine and organic moral order, represented by the Church but equally present as a living, unifying force in each and every individual making up that Church, is accompanied by what Dostoyevsky considered its antithesis: the perversion of Christianity into Roman Catholicism, where the Church's ecclesiastical authority demands the acquiescence of the individual in what is essentially a hierarchical, temporal and coercive structure. As Alyosha observes, Ivan presents his arguments with an unexpected modesty and restraint. Richard Peace has argued that this reticence is a deliberate ploy which allows Ivan to sustain and exploit the profound ambiguity of his idea. Ivan is playing a clever game in the Elder's cell, allowing others (the landowner Myusov and Father Paisy) to advocate the opposing poles of his dialectic (*Dostoyevsky: An Examination*). Equally importantly, we witness much of this key scene through Alyosha's eyes, and it is entirely likely that the innocent novice, moved by his brother's apparent support for the Church, fails to pick up and convey any note of irony present in Ivan's disquisition.

When Zosima himself eventually intervenes in the debate, it is apparently to corroborate Ivan's conclusions, but there is something in the Elder's demeanour which suggests that he is not taking Ivan's words at their face value. His unease is well founded, for as the novel develops it emerges that Ivan's views on the Church and State have been an ironic preparation for the disclosure of his real views in his unwritten 'poem', 'The Grand Inquisitor'. The same dialectic that produces the thesis of the State-turned-Church also yields the antithesis of the Inquisitor's monstrous Church-turned-State. Ivan's apparent advocacy of the former presupposes faith in God's grace and acceptance of His moral order; otherwise, the whole idea of the State-turned-Church is a nonsensical delusion. Yet it quickly becomes clear that Ivan's personal convictions do not rest on the acceptance of divine grace, but on the ideal of the rebellious personality and the proclamation that if God's order is discarded then 'everything is permitted'. It is Myusov who gleefully reveals to the assembled company the extent of Ivan's 'paradoxical' nature:

Not more than five days ago, at a certain social gathering here, consisting mainly of ladies, he [Ivan] solemnly announced in the course of an argument that there was decidedly nothing in the whole wide world to make men love their fellow men, no natural law that man should love mankind, and that if love did exist on earth it was not as the result of a natural law, but simply because people believed in immortality ... and that if you were to destroy mankind's belief in immortality, then not only love but every living force capable of sustaining earthly life would dry up at once. Not only that, there would then be no immorality: everything would be permitted, even cannibalism.   (Book II, Ch. 5)

These disclosures reveal the significance of Zosima's earlier intervention, when he insisted that justice and punishment were spiritual realities inextricably woven into the individual's conscience. Zosima's words represent the opening skirmish in an ideological conflict that continues throughout the novel, culminating in the section 'Pro and Contra'; they are an early challenge to what is subsequently to become Ivan's unambiguous advocacy of the enforced and temporal order of the Church-turned-State.

Although Ivan's article clearly echoes arguments found in Solovyov's thought, its critique of the pagan nature of Western European civilisation suggests that Dostoyevsky also drew upon what he knew of the Slavophile analysis of history. The Slavophiles had identified Roman Catholicism, the classical heritage of the pagan Roman state, and a political order arising from the violence of conquest, as the three strands that had determined the nature of European civilisation; and they argued that in both Western society and the Catholic Church harmonious order and 'justice' could be achieved only through the forcible suppression of individual freedom, a concept most effectively illustrated in Ivan Karamazov's legend, 'The Grand Inquisitor'.

The exposition of this 'poem' to Alyosha marks the culmination of Ivan's rebellion. It is preceded by a telling scene in which Ivan extracts from his brother the confession that he too would not consent to erect the edifice of human happiness upon the suffering of an innocent child. For a moment Ivan thinks that he has drawn his brother into complicity in his revolt, but there is an abyss between the two here: Ivan's refusal marks a rejection of God's justice and order, Alyosha's a rejection of man's. He will not trespass upon God's domain, arguing that only the Lord has the right to forgive, to judge, and to erect a moral order. In this way the scene is set for 'The Grand Inquisitor'. The action of Ivan's poem takes place in sixteenth-century Seville, at the height of the Spanish Inquisition, when heretics and opponents of the Catholic Church are daily consigned to the flames. Amidst the carnage Christ returns to earth, not in the promised Second Coming, but in order momentarily to re-inspire his children. The Grand Inquisitor, a grizzled and embittered old man, witnesses Christ as once more he moves among men performing miracles and stirring hearts, offering compassion and love to those who have known only fear. Ivan dramatically depicts the Inquisitor's reactions:

He stops in front of the crowd and observes from a distance. He has seen everything. He has seen the coffin set down at *his* feet and the young girl raised from the dead, and his face darkens. He knits his grey, bushy brows and his eyes flash with an ominous fire. He stretches forth his finger and commands the guards to seize *him*. And behold, such is his power and so accustomed are the people to obey him, so humbled and meekly submissive are they, that the crowd immediately parts before the guards, who, in the deathly silence that suddenly descends, lay their hands on *him* and lead him away.

(Book V, Ch. 5)

The moment resonates in the chamber of the novel. The Inquisitor has witnessed the miracles and has recognised the presence of that Christ in whose name his Church acts. Yet he rejects and turns against his Lord, reasoning that Christ's reappearance threatens the order established by the Church on the basis of fear and obedience. With the command to arrest Christ, the Inquisitor's reason prevails over his heart and senses, and the parallel with Ivan's rejection of his instinctive love of God's creation, also dictated by intellect, is inescapable. The Inquisitor explains his position, essentially a parabolic reformulation of Ivan's own rebellion, later that night in the cell where Christ is confined. Ivan invests his account of this scene with a tantalising ambiguity by suggesting that it might be merely the product of an old man's delirium. The suggestion is enough to lend this encounter between a self-confessed disciple of satanic revolt and a possibly hallucinatory Christ a rich artistic meaning: it prepares the way for Ivan's later, contrapuntal encounter with an hallucinatory devil. Such examples of echoing, pre-echoing and 'situation rhyme' (when details from one scene may be recognised in another) are an essential part of the architectural cohesion of *The Brothers Karamazov*.

In Christ's cell, on this hot Seville night 'heavy with the scent of laurel and lemon', the old Inquisitor finally speaks out and 'says aloud what he has kept silent for ninety years'. 'Why have you come to meddle with us?' he asks Christ, and receiving no answer he vows to burn his prisoner at the stake 'as the vilest of heretics'. He sets out his conviction that Christ's gift of freedom of faith to mankind and his advocacy of the

Kingdom of God for those who deserve it have deprived mankind of its only real chance of happiness in a strictly ordered
paradise on earth. By offering man harmony, redemption and
justice in the next world, Christ denied him these blessings in
this one, condemning him instead to a history of enmity, chaos,
and moral and social disorder. It fell to the Catholic Church,
argues the Inquisitor, to take over Christ's ministry, and for
centuries it has in Christ's name been engaged in the systematic
task of correcting his work by retrieving the freedom he
bestowed. Man, according to the Inquisitor, is a weak and
rebellious creature, for whom freedom is unendurable; his
happiness is incompatible with freedom:

Instead of gaining possession of man's freedom, you gave him even
more! Or did you forget that peace of mind and even death are dearer
to man than free choice in the knowledge of good and evil? There
is nothing more alluring to man than his freedom of conscience,
but there is nothing more tormenting either. And instead of firm
foundations for settling man's conscience once and for all, you chose
everything that was extraordinary, enigmatic and vague, you chose
everything that was beyond man's capabilities, thereby acting as though
you did not love man at all – you, who came to give his life for him!
Instead of seizing his freedom, you multiplied it and burdened the
spiritual kingdom of man with its torments forever. You wanted man's
free love so that he should follow you freely, fascinated and captivated
by you. Instead of the strict ancient law, man had in future to decide
for himself with a free heart what was good and what was evil, having
only your image before him as a guide. But did it really not occur
to you that he would end by renouncing and questioning even your
image and your truth, if he were oppressed by such a burden as
freedom of choice?   (Book V, Ch. 5)

The Inquisitor's arguments for a temporal order designed to
lift the burden of freedom and to bestow, by force if necessary,
the gifts of harmony and happiness pivot upon his interpretation of Christ's temptations in the wilderness:

The terrible and wise spirit, the spirit of self-annihilation and non-
being… spoke with you in the wilderness, and it is said in the scriptures that he 'tempted' you. Is that so? And could anything truer
have been said than what he revealed to you in his three questions
and what you spurned, what are referred to in the scriptures as

'temptations'? And yet if there has ever been on earth a fully real and prodigious miracle, then it was on that day, on the day of those three temptations. (Book V, Ch. 5)

The Inquisitor goes on to explain that such was the wisdom of those three temptations that they revealed to Christ the secret of the only forces capable of bringing about paradise on earth: 'There are three forces, the only three forces on earth able to conquer and hold captive forever the conscience of these weak rebels, for the sake of their own happiness — these forces are: miracle, mystery and authority'. It was, of course, precisely because these were *forces*, designed to coerce, that Christ rejected them, leaving man with freedom of choice. It says much for the architectural integrity of *The Brothers Karamazov* that Dostoyevsky even manages to weave oblique references to his main plot into the Inquisitor's account of Christ's temptations. The fact is that in the wilderness Christ resisted the same three temptations to which the Karamazov brothers yield in the course of the novel. The first of Christ's temptations occurs when Satan suggests that he transform the stones of the desert into loaves, thereby gaining man's allegiance both by the force of mystery and by the immediate gratification of his physical wants. Christ refuses, asserting that man does not live by bread alone and that the satisfaction of his physical needs is meaningless unless his spiritual needs are also met. This, of course, echoes the dilemma of Dmitry, whose physical appetites are chaotic and destructive in the absence of a guiding spiritual principle. Before his moral conversion Dmitry tries to live by bread alone, seeking oblivion in sensual gratification.

In the next temptation Satan suggests that Christ leap down from a pinnacle of the temple, so that God might save him and men might be converted by the miraculous. Christ again refuses, this time on the grounds that men must come to him of their own free will and not be compelled by the force of a miracle. Moreover, Christ recognises that by precipitating himself from the temple he would be tempting God and testing his faith, when faith in God must be stronger than any miraculous proof. The significance of this temptation is revealed by Alyosha's loss of faith when God fails to crown Zosima's life with the miracle all had been expecting. Christ builds his Church on the same grounds that cause Alyosha's failure of faith — the absence of a miracle.

Finally, Christ is offered direct dominion over all the kingdoms of the earth — the sword of Caesar — and the opportunity to create a tangible, temporal, 'Euclidean' harmony by direct rule, in order to overcome — by authority and not by love — the bestial discords of human existence. Christ refuses, again insisting that men should be free to exercise choice in the face of good and evil. Ivan, though, longs for such a concrete, secular order and the imposition of harmony through force, as his poem 'The Grand Inquisitor' testifies. The Inquisitor's account of this third temptation discloses his true nature: he and his Church are the products of a pagan civilisation, demanding unity without freedom and sacrificing the ideal of a divine order based on God's love to the lower, but more tangible order created through political force. He makes it clear that he and those with him have transferred their allegiances from Christ to the Devil:

And shall I hide our secret from you? Perhaps you actually want to hear it from my lips? Listen then: we are not with you but with *him* and that's our secret! We have been with him and not with you for a long time, for eight centuries. Exactly eight centuries ago we took from him what you rejected with indignation, that last gift he offered you having shown you all the kingdoms of the earth. We took from him Rome and the sword of Caesar and proclaimed ourselves the kings of the earth.   (Book V, Ch. 5)

The Inquisitor's reference to eight centuries is precise and significant. He dates the process of man's salvation not from Christ's ministry, but from the Catholic Church's emergence as a political force. Ivan's 'poem' is set in the sixteenth century and it was eight centuries earlier, in 756, that Rome proclaimed itself a theocratic state and assumed temporal authority, thus betraying Christ's legacy and his insistence that 'My Kingdom is not of this world'. Dostoyevsky commented directly on this process of betrayal when he introduced a reading of 'The Grand Inquisitor' to the students of St Petersburg University in December 1879: 'If you distort Christ's faith by combining it with worldly aims, you immediately lose the whole meaning of Christianity, the mind must undoubtedly fall into unbelief, and in place of Christ's great ideal there arises only a new tower of Babylon. Christianity's elevated view of mankind is debased into seeing it as a herd of swine, and under the appearance of *social* love for mankind there appears a barely disguised contempt for it' (XV, 198).

Dostoyevsky's words remind us that there is another dimension to 'The Grand Inquisitor'. It is hardly likely that Ivan, a young radical intellectual of the 1860s, should devote such effort merely in order to justify the temporal aspirations of the Roman Church. It is not Catholicism he is advocating, and Dostoyevsky implicitly refuting, in the arguments of his Inquisitor: it is socialism and the struggle for a 'just' and stable political order. For Dostoyevsky there was in any case little to choose between Catholicism and socialism. Both represented the utopian's delusion: the misplaced belief that paradise on earth can replace God's paradise, that earthly bread can taste as sweet as the bread of heaven, and that political structures, rather than Christian love, can create the brotherhood of man. Catholicism and socialism merge in the political dream of Ivan's old Inquisitor; this sixteenth-century Spanish cardinal somehow manages to refer obliquely to the British socialist, Robert Owen (1771–1858), in words close to those used in Alexander Herzen's treatment of Owen in his memoirs, *My Past and Thoughts*: 'Do you know that centuries will pass and mankind will proclaim through the lips of its wisdom and science that there is no crime, and therefore no sin, but that there are only starving people. "Feed them first and then demand virtue of them!" — that's what will be written on the banners they will raise against you and with which they will destroy your temple' (Book V, Ch. 5). Owen too proclaimed the virtue of man and ascribed his sufferings to a Christianity which, in the name of some mythical happiness in the next world, denied him justice in this.

For Dostoyevsky, though, the problem with socialist attempts to create world harmony on the basis of social rather than Christian love was that such attempts were more likely to end in tyranny than in justice. As he indicated in his comments to the students at St Petersburg University, social love proclaims a love for humanity in the abstract, but it often conceals contempt for the individual in particular. The differences between social and Christian love form a recurrent motif in *The Brothers Karamazov* and are first introduced in a discussion between Liza's mother Mrs Khokhlakova and Father Zosima. The Elder cites the example of a doctor he once knew:

'I love mankind', he said, 'but I do surprise myself: the more I love mankind in general, the less I love people in particular, that is separately, as separate individuals. In my dreams I often entertain passionate plans for serving humanity and would perhaps actually go to the cross for people if it were suddenly demanded of me. But, on the other hand, I know from experience that I am not capable of living in the same room as someone else for two days on end ... I become an enemy of the people as soon as they touch me. Nevertheless, it has always happened that the more I hated people as individuals, the more ardent my love for humanity at large became.'

(Book II, Ch. 4)

Such social love (or romantic love, as Zosima calls it) provides an inadequate basis for heaven on earth, with the result that utopian socialist dreams are inevitably corrupted into political tyranny. 'The Grand Inquisitor' illustrates this and provides a startlingly prescient anticipation of those modern totalitarian states that have been erected in the name of human freedom, justice and equality. Certainly one can discern the seeds of political 'doublethink', as well as of Stalin's thought control, in the following example of the Inquisitor's sophistry and recognition of the provisional nature of truth. He is describing the submissive future subjects of his authoritarian Church-turned-State:

In receiving loaves from us they will, of course, clearly see that we are taking these loaves, made by their own hands, from them in order to distribute them back to them with no miracle involved at all. They will see that we have not turned stones into loaves, but they will in truth be more pleased at receiving them from our hands than at getting the bread itself! For they will remember only too well that before, without us, the very bread they made turned to stones in their hands, but that when they turned to us the very stones turned to loaves in their hands!

(Book V, Ch. 5)

This is a remarkably accurate anticipation of the psychology of the totalitarian state, and the fact that the Inquisitor's prophetic vision has been realised so terribly in the twentieth century says much for the truth of Ivan's insight into human nature. Indeed, Dostoyevsky himself suspected that, on the level of ideas, at least, he had given the Devil all the best tunes in this critical section of his novel. The ending of Ivan's poem, when a silent Christ kisses the Inquisitor on his 'bloodless, aged lips' and the startled old man impulsively lets his captive go, is touching and poetic, but it inadequately counters the force of the Inquisitor's arguments. Dostoyevsky's friend Pobedonostsev recognised this in a letter to the author dated 16 August 1879: 'Your "Grand Inquisitor" has made a very powerful impression on me. Rarely have I read anything so powerful. Only I have been waiting and wondering where the refutation, rejoinder and elucidation will come from'. Dostoyevsky always intended there to be such a refutation of Ivan's views, as he explained in a letter to Lyubimov of 10 May 1879: 'My hero's blasphemy will be triumphantly refuted in the next (June) number on which I am now working with fear, trepidation and awe, for I consider my task (the rout of anarchism) a civic deed' (XXX/1, 64). Like Pobedonostsev, however, he recognised that it would be no straightforward matter to counter Ivan's compelling and logically impeccable rebellion against divine order. He wrote to Pobedonostsev on 24 August 1879, revealing his fears: 'In this there lies all my concern and all my unease, for I have intended this sixth book, "A Russian Monk", which is due on August 31, to be a reply to this entire *negative side*. Therefore I tremble for it, wondering if it will be a *sufficient* reply. The more so since it is an indirect reply, not one which takes up point by point propositions expressed earlier (in "The Grand Inquisitor" and before); it is therefore oblique. It presents something diametrically opposed to the world view expressed earlier − but once again, it is not presented point by point, but as an artistic picture, so to speak. This is what worries me: will I make myself clear and will I achieve even a small part of my aim?' (XXX/1, 122).

Dostoyevsky thus conceived 'A Russian Monk', which

contains extracts from the life and teachings of the Elder
Zosima, as an oblique response to Ivan's rebellion, as an
'artistic picture' which indirectly affirms the superiority of
God's moral order to that erected by man in his intellectual
pride. Its very indirectness helps to explain why many com-
mentators have found it inadequate and out of place, despite
Dostoyevsky's insistence that it formed the 'culminating point'
of his novel. The aim Dostoyevsky set himself in this book
was a dauntingly difficult one: to counter his own all-too-
realistic depiction of contemporary nihilism with an example
of Christian virtue that was simultaneously iconic and mimetic.
Comments in his letters make it clear that he hoped to create
a figure that would affirm the Christian ideals without violating
the verisimilitude of the realistic novel. 'Like it or not', he
wrote to Pobedonostsev, 'artistic considerations demand that
I include in the biography of my monk even the most banal
aspects, in order not to offend against artistic realism' (XXX/1,
122). Earlier, he had written to Lyubimov explaining that
'A Russian Monk' would not be a sermon but 'a tale of real
life', merging moral idealism and artistic truth and thus
triumphantly demonstrating 'that the pure, ideal Christian is
not something abstract, but is concretely real and possible
before our eyes' (XXX/1, 68).

Discussion of whether Dostoyevsky succeeds in this aim,
and whether the inclusion of 'A Russian Monk' within *The
Brothers Karamazov* is appropriate, demands consideration
of both the content and the form of this Book. For the non-
Orthodox reader it is the content of Zosima's biography and
teachings that affords most difficulties. His biography appears
to offer little more than several conventional, psychologically
unsubstantiated parables of spiritual rebirth, while his teachings
seem to mingle restatements of Orthodox doctrine with some
decidedly non-Orthodox opinions on Mother—Earth venera-
tion, paradise on earth, divine elation, the cult of tears, and
mutual forgiveness and responsibility. No matter how successfully dressed up in an 'artistic picture', such ideas form a wholly
indigestible course for the reader whose polemical appetite has
been whetted by Ivan Karamazov's arguments. Indeed, in

resorting to an 'artistic picture' Dostoyevsky appears to have conceded the intellectual high ground to his creature, Ivan. The problem Dostoyevsky faced in 'A Russian Monk' — and the reason he shrank from a point-by-point refutation of Ivan — was the same one he faced in the Epilogue to *Crime and Punishment*: how to depict in words the mystery of faith and salvation? Dostoyevsky recognised that he could counter Ivan's Euclidean arguments against God's order only with the 'non-Euclidean' answer of Zosima's life and teachings. The analysis of doubt is countered with an image of faith, intellect is refuted by mystery and emotion. The question is, though, whether such 'non-Euclidean' arguments belong in the 'Euclidean' world of the analytical, psychological novel; for those readers most likely to have been shaken by Ivan's arguments are also the least likely to be persuaded by the icon of Zosima. The gulf between unbelief and belief remains unbridged. For the sceptical intellect the affirmations of Zosima must remain, like Raskolnikov's conversion, a 'pious lie' (Mochulsky, *Dostoevsky: His Life and Work*), the barely concealed attempt of a desperate novelist to nudge his reader into God's camp.

In 'A Russian Monk', then, Dostoyevsky's professed desire to show his readers the way to the Church is shipwrecked on the inadequacy of the realistic novel as a vehicle for religious or moral persuasion. The strength of this genre lies in the subjecting of experience to analysis. The affirmation of faith and the presentation of the ideal require something quite different: the synthesis afforded by the poetic image. It is largely for this reason that 'A Russian Monk' — an 'artistic picture' defying analysis — strains against the novelistic form which contains it and appears to be 'segregated from the narration proper' (Hackel, 'The Religious Dimension'). It is static and assertive, rather than dynamic and revelatory. In the novel proper, truth about the characters and what they represent emerges from dramatic verbal or psychological clashes, such as the scandalous scene in the monastery (Book II), where the personalities of all present are disclosed in their reactions to the encounter between the shameless Fyodor Pavlovich and the saintly Zosima, or the marvellous meeting between Alyosha and Ivan, as the latter reveals the extent of his rebellion. The 'truth' of 'A Russian Monk' is, on the contrary, presented in the form of indigestible tract and parable, apparently untouched by the narrative devices of the novelist. As we shall see, the presentation of Ivan's point of view in 'The Grand Inquisitor' is undermined by the Romantic rhetoric with which Dostoyevsky invests it. No such irony or paradox are allowed to challenge the supremacy of the Elder's voice or to violate the beliefs he expresses:

'He who does not believe in God will not believe in God's people. But he who has faith in God's people will also behold His Glory, even though he had not believed in it hitherto. Only the common people and their coming spiritual power will convert our atheists, who have torn themselves away from their native soil.'

(Book VI, Ch. 2)

These words have all the confident, unassailable authority of a sermon from the pulpit, and, in a sense, this is what they are. The comments on the spiritual power of God's people to restore the alienated intellectual should alert us to the fact that we are here in the presence not so much of Zosima, a fictional character, as of Dostoyevsky, the moral and social preacher.

On the other hand, Dostoyevsky *the novelist* seems at first to drop out of the picture altogether in this Book, as if he senses that he has no place here. He painstakingly creates distance by interposing thick layers of narrative insulation between himself as author and the incidents described in 'A Russian Monk'. For a start he introduces a startlingly different narrative form with a new author, deliberately recreating the traditional hagiographic genre of the 'Spiritual Life', or *Zhitiye*, as used in the Russian 'Lives of the Saints', and even borrowing freely from earlier models. Moreover, it is Alyosha Karamazov who has composed this *zhitiye*, painstakingly taking down Zosima's words or recreating them from memory. Dostoyevsky goes out of his way to stress, however, that Alyosha's role is much more than merely that of the scribe or chronicler: it is truly *authorial*. The young novice avails himself of such narrative stratagems as the disruption of chronological sequence, the reporting of speech out of context, and the weaving of uninterrupted narrative out of fragmentary recollections. What is more, within Alyosha's *zhitiye* other narrators play their part: Zosima tells the story of his past and the spiritual rebirth of his brother; the Mysterious Visitor recounts his own criminal past, as well as his path to enlightenment and contrition. These various narrative 'layers' allow Dostoyevsky the opportunity to slip away unnoticed from the scene of that most heinous of the novelist's crimes – direct and overt moral idealism and didacticism.

The novelist is not, however, totally overpowered by the preacher. Enough of him remains to ensure that even if 'A Russian Monk' violates the integrity of *The Brothers Karamazov* by its genre, narrative structure and moral didacticism, it does not wholly vitiate the novel's architectural design. Through the devices of character echoing and situation rhyme it is in fact skilfully keyed into the novel's primary plot – the lives and beliefs of the brothers Karamazov. This must be explored in some detail.

Alyosha's 'manuscript' is divided into two main sections, occupying chapters two and three of 'A Russian Monk'. Chapter two deals with Zosima's biography; chapter three with his teachings. Each of these chapters is in turn subdivided, and each of the subdivisions shows itself to be particularly relevant to the experience of one of the Karamazov brothers, although each contains material that bears upon the other brothers too. The first subdivision of chapter two is designed primarily to evoke Alyosha and his experience. In it Zosima describes the life, religious transfiguration and early death of his elder brother Markel, of whom, he remarks, Alyosha constantly reminds him. As is to be the case with Alyosha after Zosima's death, Markel is rescued from the abyss of unbelief by an ecstatic revelation of the beauty and harmony of God's universe, and, like Alyosha in his dealings with Snegiryov, Markel also flirts with the heresy of utopianism – the belief that if only we wished it enough, paradise could be established on earth. Moreover, he expresses his sense of paradise and universal harmony in the same image Alyosha associates with memories of his mother: the slanting rays of the setting sun. Markel's sense of paradise also aligns him with Dmitry, for he is acutely aware of how his own imperfect presence dishonours the glory of God's creation. Furthermore, his own history — he was once a freethinking rebel whose logic predisposed him against creation — clearly echoes Ivan's.

Ivan though is most clearly brought to mind in the second subdivision of chapter two. Here Zosima's profession of admiration for the biblical story of Job provides a barely concealed counterpoint to Ivan's rebellion against divine justice. Job's faith withstands the test imposed by God: the loss of his wealth, cattle and children. The fact that the meaning of this 'test' remains unclear increases the greatness of the story, according to Zosima: 'But it is great just because there is a mystery here: eternal truth and its transient earthly image are brought together here. Before earthly justice the act of eternal justice is accomplished' (Book VI, Ch. 2). Unlike Ivan's, Job's love of God and creation is more important than his understanding of them, and the fact that his 'test' turns upon the same pivot as Ivan's rebellion — the sufferings of innocent children, in Job's case his own — makes the linkage clearer, as does the echo of Ivan's article on ecclesiastical courts contained in Zosima's words. Ivan's dilemma, and Alyosha's earlier advice that he love life regardless of reason, are also to be discerned in Zosima's observation, 'Every blade of grass, every tiny insect, ant, golden bee, all of them know so wondrously their path, without possessing reason'.

The third subdivision of chapter two, where Zosima recounts his experiences as an army officer, completes the symmetry by providing an oblique commentary on the life of Dmitry. Zosima's description of his younger self as a reckless, 'almost savage creature', his predilection for drunkenness, debauchery and dashing behaviour, his inheritance of a sum of money, and his determination to plunge himself without restraint into the pleasures of life, all recall Dmitry. The young Zosima's love of books echoes Dmitry's intoxication with poetry, and both share a Schilleresque love of beauty. When Zosima describes his attachment to 'a young and beautiful girl, intelligent and worthy, of noble and pure character, the daughter of a highly respected family', who is in fact in love with another, we see the outlines of Dmitry's relationship with Katerina. The young Zosima's assault on his servant Afanasy brings to mind Dmitry's attack on Grigory, and when he subsequently seeks Afanasy's forgiveness by bowing to the ground before him, his chronologically later bow before Dmitry is grotesquely anticipated. Zosima's 'conversion', as he prepares to shed blood in a duel, also parallels Dmitry's: just as Dmitry is prevented by a feeling of shame and disgrace from carrying out the murder of his father, so Zosima is unable to go through with the duel. The beauty of the morning, the feeling that he alone impairs this beauty, and a sudden realisation that each man is responsible for others, all accompany Zosima's change of heart, just as they do Dmitry's.

These variations on the novel's main themes continue into the fourth and final subdivision of Zosima's biography, the tale of the mysterious visitor who has murdered the woman he loves and who eventually confesses to the crime some fourteen years later. The description of the murder and its aftermath evokes several echoes from the Dmitry plot. The victim, to whom the mystery man is passionately drawn, refuses to marry him because she is pledged to another, an officer on active service whom she expects to return soon. These details compare with Dmitry's passion for Grushenka and her faithfulness to her Pole. After the crime the true murderer escapes suspicion, but an innocent servant is apprehended — intoxicated and covered in blood. This inverts Dmitry's fate, when he is arrested though innocent, and the guilty servant, Smerdyakov, escapes suspicion. The fate of Ivan is also anticipated in the mysterious visitor's tale: he first refuses to confess and submit to God's justice because it would involve the suffering of innocent children, those of his own family, who would share his disgrace. Also like Ivan, he eventually tries to confess publicly to the crime and nobody believes him, whereupon he succumbs to brain fever and his actions are ascribed to a mental breakdown.

The primary significance of the tale of the mysterious visitor, however, lies in the way it picks up and modulates the novel's central preoccupation with the fragmentation of contemporary life. Echoing the belief expressed by Zosima, Alyosha, Dmitry

and others, that paradise is there for the taking if only we
wished it enough, Zosima's visitor argues that the path to this
paradise is blocked only by man's *isolation*. This isolation
prevents him achieving the fullness of life, it inhibits true
brotherhood and community of effort, and it leads ultimately
to self-destruction. Not only do we see here the novel's dominant themes, we also see their source: the thought of Nikolay
Fyodorov. The visitor's words could almost be a quotation
from *Philosophy of the Common Task*:

Until you actually become everyone's brother, the brotherhood of
man will not come to pass ... For [man] has become accustomed to
relying on himself alone and has separated himself from the whole
as a self-contained unit. He has taught his heart not to believe in
the help of other men, in people and in mankind, and he is only
afraid that he will lose his money and the rights he has acquired for
himself. Everywhere nowadays the mind of man has begun ironically
to overlook the fact that the true security of the individual lies not
in his own isolated effort but in the common solidarity of people.
                                                              (Book VI, Ch. 2)

The novel's answer to such isolation, as clarified in the experiences of Ivan, Dmitry and Alyosha, lies in the destruction
of the fragmented, autonomous, rebellious, self-centred individual and the birth of the God-man, characterised by love,
self-sacrifice, and the sense of universal responsibility. This
need for the old to die in order that the new might emerge is
proclaimed by the novel's epigraph, a quotation from the
Gospel of St John, and this too re-emerges in Zosima's tale
of his mysterious visitor: 'Verily, verily, I say unto you, Except
a corn of wheat fall into the ground and die, it abideth alone:
but if it die, it bringeth forth much fruit'. Like the brothers
Karamazov, the mysterious visitor redeems himself through
suffering and finds his salvation along the road to Calvary.
    The second part of Alyosha's 'manuscript', consisting of
Zosima's discourses on monasticism, brotherhood, love,
equality, prayer, humility, mercy, judgement and hell, also
seeks to legitimate itself artistically by striking in the reader
chords of recognition of events, themes and characters in the
novel proper. Thus Zosima's advocacy of the contemplative

isolation of the monastic way of life, which is a form of worship of God's creation, is offered as a counterpoint to the novel's preoccupation with the godless and rebellious isolation of contemporary man. His insistence that man's quest for freedom without God must lead to slavery affords an answer to Ivan's Inquisitor, as does his belief that man must love his brother even in his weakness and sinfulness. Indeed, despite Dostoyevsky's protestations to the contrary, there are moments when Zosima's discourses appear to be a point-by-point refutation of the arguments comprising Ivan's rebellion. We hear a travesty of Ivan's idea when Zosima protests against the exploitation of the young in factories: 'There must be no more of this, monks, there must be no more torturing of children' (Book VI, Ch. 3). We see Ivan also in Zosima's characterisation of the educated classes: 'Following science, they wish to erect a just life on the basis of their reason alone, but no longer with Christ as before, and they have already proclaimed that there is no such thing as crime, no such thing as sin. And they are right in their own way, for if you don't have God how can you have crime?' (Book VI, Ch. 3).

The novel's main theme of the illegitimacy of the Karamazov family, culminating in parricide, is suggested in Zosima's words about servants: 'Why should my servant not be like a relative of mine, so that I accept him finally into my family and rejoice at this?' Here we see not only an implied comment on Smerdyakov's role as the excluded bastard son through whom the Karamazov poisons seep, but we also sense a reference to Dmitry's relationship with Grigory Kutuzov. There are many other examples of such 'recapitulation' in Zosima's discourses – far too many to explore fully here: there is an echo of Grushenka's legend of the onion in Zosima's remark that it is good to have someone to intercede and pray for oneself; the Elder's comments on hell recall Fyodor Pavlovich's fascination with the same subject; and his belief in universal solidarity and contact with other worlds is couched in terms similar to Alyosha's mystical revelation after the Cana of Galilee episode.

Through such devices 'A Russian Monk' is bound to the rest of *The Brothers Karamazov*, but it never really belongs.

It remains a cuckoo in the nest, a piece of artistic sleight-of-hand, testifying to Dostoyevsky's belief in an overriding divine order without ever becoming a satisfactory answer to Ivan's rejection of that order in the preceding Book. In this novel, as in those which came before it, Dostoyevsky fails to rise, as perhaps he must, to the challenge of incorporating the mystery of faith and salvation within the limits of realistic art.

'A realist in a higher sense'

Dostoyevsky's attempts to disguise 'A Russian Monk' as a legitimate component of a realistic novel, as well as his comments to Pobedonostsev on the need 'not to offend against artistic realism', raise the question of just how 'realistic' his art is. In this respect, rarely has a major artist aroused such controversy as that evoked by Dostoyevsky's works. For a long time it was fashionable, both in Russia and the West, to regard him as a great philosopher, publicist and ideologue, but as a haphazard and seriously flawed novelist whose pretensions to realism did not stand comparison with those of his great contemporaries like Tolstoy, Turgenev and Goncharov. The circumstances under which he wrote — the haste, the pressing financial and journalistic deadlines, the gambling mania, the epileptic fits, the polemical urgency — all conspired to reinforce the impression that his novels were rushed, imperfect and ill-crafted structures designed to meet immediate needs rather than the timeless requirements of art. This view was first seriously challenged only after the Bolshevik revolution with the opening of the Dostoyevsky archives and the publication of his meticulous notebook and draft materials, which showed the care, judgement and craftsmanship that accompanied the process of composition. Not all were convinced: Vladimir Nabokov in particular persisted in seeing Dostoyevsky as a mediocre sensationalist from the Gothic stable ('Fyodor Dostoevski'), and the suspicion of melodramatic excess and artistic carelessness has continued to hang over Dostoyevsky's reputation among his critics.

Critical scepticism about Dostoyevsky's credentials as a great realistic novelist (scepticism to be examined in the next chapter) is clearly at odds with the writer's own frequently expressed conviction that his work was in the fullest sense true to life. In its simplest form this conviction was rooted in Dostoyevsky's concern that his art should incorporate the stuff of reality. He drew much of his material from newspaper accounts and took pains to check the accuracy of details. For example, the early drafts for *The Brothers Karamazov* contain such queries as: 'Find out if it is possible to lie between the rails under a railway carriage travelling at full speed', 'Find out whether the wife *of a convicted prisoner* can marry someone else straight away' and 'Check up on child labour in factories' (XV, 199). On a deeper level Dostoyevsky's view emerged from his belief that realistic art should achieve more than the mere depiction of the surface appearances of life: it should probe the deeper structures of society. It is clear from his correspondence that Dostoyevsky considered most contemporary 'realists' to have failed in this respect: 'I have entirely different notions of reality and realism than our realists and critics,' he wrote to A. N. Maykov in 1868, 'With their kind of realism one cannot explain so much as a hundredth part of the real facts which have actually occurred. But with our idealism we have even prophesied facts' (XXVIII/2, 329). In an undated comment in his notebooks he described himself as 'a realist in a higher sense' (XXVII, 65). If this 'higher realism' appeared to flout the conventions of verisimilitude established in traditional realism – where an emphasis on common experience, social ritual, physical description, along with an avoidance of the extreme and the exotic, served to sustain the illusion of normal life – then this merely spotlighted the inadequacy of that tradition: 'I have my own view of reality (in art),' he wrote to his friend N. Strakhov in 1869, 'and what most people regard as fantastic and exceptional is sometimes for me the very essence of reality. Everyday trivialities and a conventional view of them, in my opinion, not only fall short of realism but are even contrary to it' (XXIX/1, 19).

The core of Dostoyevsky's ideas on the nature of realism
and its relationship to reality may be found in entries in *The
Diary of a Writer* for 1877, where, as we have seen, he comments
on Tolstoy's achievements in *Anna Karenina*. His rejection
of the stability of Tolstoy's moral vision was accompanied by
a rejection of the artistic forms that sustained that vision
of stability. An artistic structure like *Anna Karenina*, which
suggested order where there was only discord and which concealed the shifting uncertainties of reality behind an illusion
of artistic order and normality, ignored the primary task of
realistic art: to capture not just the appearances but also the
spirit of the age. Dostoyevsky clearly felt that the 'realist'
must sometimes sacrifice verisimilitude, the preoccupation
solely with the appearances of reality, in order to express
its spirit. He wrote in *The Idiot* of the novelist's duty 'to
select social types and present them in artistic form: types
remarkably rarely encountered as such in real life, but which
are almost more real than reality itself' (VIII, 383). The pursuit
of such 'higher realism' led Dostoyevsky to devise new novelistic
forms, a whole aesthetics of uncertainty, to match the instability
of the age they were designed to depict: forms in which deep
probing into the innermost and darkest recesses of the human
soul took the place of portraiture and *paysage*; where coincidence, symbolism and myth took their place in the 'realistic
novel', threatening the limits of verisimilitude; where the
narrative point of view deliberately blurred the boundaries of
dream and reality, of subjective and objective; and where the
clash of ideas took place not just in the limited confines of
the conversation and the drawing room, but also in the infinite
spaces of the souls of his possessed characters.

The Brothers Karamazov illustrates perfectly these essential
features of Dostoyevsky's realism. The novel is 'dramatic', relying predominantly on dialogue and the interaction of 'voices',
and Dostoyevsky takes full advantage of the opportunities
afforded by dramatic licence. The temporal and spatial axes of
the novel are manipulated for maximum dramatic and melo-
dramatic effect: 'More action, or conversation, is compressed
into short spans of time than is physically possible ... Likewise,

space is turned into a stage, where characters who have to meet just happen to cross each other's paths. Both space and time are treated symbolically' (Terras, *A Karamazov Companion*). A fine example of such dramatic intersection is the coming together of all the novel's major protagonists, except Smerdyakov, in Zosima's cell and the subsequent scandal-scene as the values they represent clash and intermingle (Book II). The scene becomes a focal point, where slapstick humour, in the form of Fyodor's buffoonery, runs against the high drama of Dmitry's hatred; where the essential qualities of each character are disclosed and their future roles fore-shadowed; where the possibility of parricide is first raised; where the later philosophical clash between Ivan and Zosima is rehearsed; and where all is concentrated into a single, intense encounter.

Similar 'intensification' is evident in the way Dostoyevsky 'squeezes' reality for its symbolic and allegorical significance. This is not to suggest that *The Brothers Karamazov* is just an allegorical structure 'in which certain characters monopolise and are monopolised by certain attributes' (Belknap, *The Structure*). Dostoyevsky's characters are convincing inhabitants of nineteenth-century Russia, not abstractions from a medieval morality play, but they do nonetheless carry a positive allegorical and symbolic charge, both in the qualities they embody and the events they are required to enact. This study has already considered examples of how *The Brothers Karamazov* functions simultaneously on both the mimetic and mythic levels, and these confirm Peace's view that allegory is always present as a skeleton supporting the 'living flesh' of Dostoyevsky's novels (*Dostoyevsky: An Examination*). A very obvious example of how Dostoyevsky enriches the stuff of life with elements of myth is his consistent use of symbolic proper names: the town in the novel is called Skotoprigonyevsk (cattle pen); Smerdyakov's name implies a stinking abomination; Alyosha's name suggests Alexey, Man of God; Dmitry's derives from Demeter, the goddess of corn and fertility; Ivan's namesake might be St John the Merciful; and Zosima's name in Greek suggests 'life' or 'alive'.

Many critics have pointed also to the lack of physicality of Dostoyevsky's characters and of the world they inhabit as characteristic of his 'higher realism' and further evidence of his mythic rather than mimetic vision. Mirsky has claimed that 'real flesh' is conspicuously absent from Dostoyevsky's world and that his characters are atoms charged by the electricity of ideas (*Russian Literature*). Others have contrasted the absence of physicality in Dostoyevsky's novels with the sensualism and rich physical authenticity of the world created by Tolstoy. Merezhkovsky was the first to argue that Tolstoy was a 'seer of the flesh' while Dostoyevsky was the 'seer of the spirit', a view later echoed in Lampert's assertion that Tolstoy tells us what it feels like to feel, whereas Dostoyevsky tells us what it feels like to think ('Dostoevsky'). There is something in these views, although there is more representational detail in *The Brothers Karamazov* than in, say, *Crime and Punishment*, where what we know of Raskolnikov's appearance is limited to a few schematic details and where the physical topography of St Petersburg is transmuted into a psychic landscape on to which are projected the contorted shadows of the murderer's imagination. The characters and settings in *The Brothers Karamazov* do possess a physical dimension, and sometimes Dostoyevsky's use of physical detail is densely textured. Dmitry is a brooding physical presence throughout, Ivan is at times described as having a peculiarly lop-sided walk, and Fyodor Pavlovich is memorably associated in the reader's mind with his flabby sensuality, insolent eyes, bloated lips, black teeth and lewdly elongated Adam's apple. The question is not one of the presence or otherwise of such details in the novel, but of the use to which they are put. Rarely do we feel that Dostoyevsky is interested in the physical world for its own sake. Rarely is a detail of physical character description deployed merely to establish that character's corporeal credentials (like Karenin's protruding ears or habit of cracking his knuckles). Instead, external details serve a symbolic function by betraying the inner, spiritual world. The appearances of the Karamazov father and sons, described above, all bear directly on the roles prescribed for these characters in the novel's philosophical and artistic design.

Dostoyevsky's subjugation of the world of appearances to the mythography of his novel is matched by his consistent tendency to pattern reality into something he considered 'more real' and less haphazard than our normal experience of it. Neglecting the conventional demands of verisimilitude and probability, he makes overt use of coincidence, repetition and 'doubling' to lay bare the underlying myths on which his novel is erected. The schematic design of the Karamazov family, the complementary nature of the three brothers, and their parodistic relationship to Smerdyakov are all illustrative of this device. There are many other examples: sometimes Dostoyevsky suggests his central themes of mutual responsibility and the communality of individuals in the human family through the 'modulation' of individual themes in a network of variations. For instance, the theme of the suffering of children, so central a component of Ivan's rebellion, is picked up and significantly modified in Dmitry's dream of the suffering babe, in Alyosha's friendship with the terminally ill Ilyusha Snegiryov, in comments made by Zosima, and in Liza Khokhlakova's twisted desire — as recounted to a bemused Alyosha — to eat pineapple compote while witnessing a child's crucifixion (Book XI, Ch. 3). Likewise, the theme of devils recurs persistently throughout the novel. Alyosha speaks of his conviction that devils have taken possession of the younger generation (Book X, Ch. 6), Father Ferapont sees devils lurking in the monastery (Book IV, Ch. 1), and even Liza confesses that she dreams of them (Book XI, Ch. 3). Such 'doubling' performs the function of knitting diverse parts of the novel together in preparation for the most important of the Devil's appearances — in Ivan's nightmare. The theme of progressive freethinking is another strand that recurs in several mutually illuminating variations. We see it in the mock grandeur of Ivan's rebellion, in the shabby cynicism of Rakitin, in the childlike naivety of the child-socialist Kolya Krasotkin's posturing, and finally in the horror of parricide as committed by Smerdyakov. Smaller details too are occasionally used by Dostoyevsky to sustain this network of inner links between discrete parts of the novel: the sum of three thousand roubles becomes a motif with a life of its own. It is the sum that Fyodor is holding as bait for Grushenka; it is the amount Dmitry appropriates from Katerina; it is the sum that all testify he spends on the night of his orgy; and it is the fee raised by Alyosha, Ivan and Katerina to pay for Dmitry's defence. Sometimes Dostoyevsky rhymes situation, rather than theme, in order to create immense architectural vaulting and to absorb his characters in the novel's central myths. For example, the dominant motif of Christ's torments and three temptations in the wilderness is paralleled by Dmitry's three torments, when he is interrogated after his arrest, by Ivan's three encounters with his tormentor, Smerdyakov, and, as Terras has suggested, by Alyosha's three 'trials' at the hands of Rakitin, Ferapont and Grushenka.

In such ways Dostoyevsky imposes a symbolic order upon the material of life. Yet does this bring into question the 'realism' of his art, as some have argued? All art, of course, involves artifice. No artist can hope simply to reproduce the shapelessness and randomness of life without subjecting it to artistic form. But whereas other 'realists' (Dostoyevsky cites Goncharov and Tolstoy by way of example) sought to reproduce the illusion of life and to create verisimilitude by disguising the artifice, Dostoyevsky's 'higher realism' appears to highlight the artificial. The resulting disclosure of allegorical and mythical skeletons beneath the 'living flesh' of the world of appearances suggests that Dostoyevsky considered truly realistic art to be revelatory rather than merely descriptive.

If this implies not just an artistic departure from what Dostoyevsky took to be the conventions of the realistic novel but also an entirely different way of looking at reality, then the same may be said of the narrative strategies he employs in *The Brothers Karamazov* and his other great works. As many critics have pointed out, Dostoyevsky's narrator in *The Brothers Karamazov* creates an indistinct and discontinuous impression and appears to possess a status 'hovering between that of a human being and that of a rhetorical device' (Belknap, *The Structure*). He is presented as a character in his own right, an inhabitant of Skotoprigonyevsk, with a 'voice' of his own and clearly separated in social and intellectual standing from the novelist himself. Yet on many occasions he appears to outgrow the function of mere chronicler and to assume the characteristics of an abstract, omniscient narrator, able to see the unseen and to report the intimate workings of the characters' minds, such as Ivan's encounter with his hallucinatory devil, the minutiae of his unwritten poem 'The Grand Inquisitor', and the details of Alyosha's ecstatic dream of the wedding at Cana. The simplest explanation for such an apparent contradiction would be to suggest that Dostoyevsky was unable to sustain consistent narrative control throughout a long novel published over a lengthy period in serial instalments: in brief, he simply forgot what his narrator could, and could not, know.

More likely, though, is Belknap's convincing suggestion that the narrative indeterminacy grew from Dostoyevsky's desire to separate the processes of expression and creation, 'making the former conspicuous in the person of the narrator, and the latter almost invisible through this interposed figure'. This opens up a matter which has been, and remains, the subject of much critical controversy. In 1929 the Soviet literary scholar, Mikhail Bakhtin, published *Problems of Dostoyevsky's Art*, a revolutionary study of Dostoyevsky's approach to the novel which remains a watershed in both Dostoyevsky criticism and literary theory. The work and its author were suppressed under Stalin, but the post-Stalin thaw saw the publication of a revised edition, *Problems of Dostoyevsky's Poetics* (1963), which has been well translated into English (Bakhtin, *Dostoyevsky's Poetics*). In this work Bakhtin claimed that Dostoyevsky had accomplished 'a small-scale Copernican revolution' by creating a wholly new novelistic form, the 'polyphonic' – multi-voiced – novel. Bakhtin's argument was that, whereas in the conventional 'monologic' novel the individual 'voices', or points of view, of the different characters were absorbed in, and modified by, the more authoritative voice of the narrator, Dostoyevsky's novels allow direct and unmodified access to the voices of his characters. The narrative voice is only one among many other, equal voices; it carries no greater authority. Just as the effect of the Copernican revolution had been to reduce the earth, until that time considered the centre of the universe, to the status of solar satellite, so the Dostoyevskian novel decentered the 'I' of the authorial or narrative voice in a genuinely pluralistic artistic world structured on the clash of fully independent voices. Put another way, the polyphonic novel rejects the omniscient, 'God's eye' narrative viewpoint assumed in Tolstoy's *Anna Karenina*. Tolstoy's narrator appears to stand outside the fictional world he describes, peering loftily into it from a vantage point none of the characters within can share. This affords the narrator, and through him the reader, a superior vision, allowing them to objectify the experiences of the fictional characters, to compare the merits of their different points of view, and to see objectively through the chaos experienced subjectively by those characters. At the end of the novel Anna can see no escape from her despair and she takes her own life. The author/narrator and the reader, however, standing on the other side of the fictional divide, can compare Anna's decline with the simultaneous growth of Kitty's happiness. They can thus see Anna's despair in a perspective denied the character herself. In this way the author/narrator is able to persuade the reader that normality finally endures and life recomposes itself. It is thus essentially the author/narrator, rather than the novel's characters, who moulds the way the reader perceives the world described in the novel.

It was Bakhtin's contention that there was no such manipulative author/narrator in the novels of Dostoyevsky. Instead, the narrator was drawn into the fictional world and condemned to the same perceptual disadvantages as the other 'voices'; the author disappeared altogether as an authoritative voice moulding the reader's interpretations and expectations; and the reader himself was left − as in real life − facing a genuine polyphony of equally weighted voices which were not arranged according to some authorial scale of values. Such a novel clearly demands a less passive and more creative reader, and it is in this respect that many of Bakhtin's critical followers have seen in the polyphonic novel the 'death' of the author and the 'birth' of the reader.

Bakhtin's analysis of Dostoyevsky's art implies much more than the recognition of a new narrative technique; it also suggests Dostoyevsky's espousal of a revolutionary and highly 'modern' way of looking at the world. When Tolstoy creates an authoritative narrative voice capable of bringing objectivity and certainty to the subjective uncertainty of the characters, he betrays his belief that such subjective uncertainty can be objectified. When he colludes with his reader in order to tell him what is really going on, he discloses his confidence in stable absolutes. For Dostoyevsky this was profoundly un-realistic, for it offered the reader a perceptual certainty and absolute objectivity he could not hope to experience in real life, where he too was a subjective participant rather than an objective spectator. Instead, Dostoyevsky's polyphonic novels, by sacrificing narrative certainty and creating a dissonant clash of independent voices, drew the reader into an artistic recreation of that very uncertainty, discord and subjective solitude which Dostoyevsky had identified as the distinguishing characteristics of his age.

Bakhtin's study of Dostoyevsky's polyphony remained general and rather abstract. Nowhere did he test his views exhaustively in a consistent, sustained analysis of one of the great novels. It is, therefore, perhaps significant that when Bakhtin's model has been applied rigorously to *The Brothers Karamazov* (and elsewhere) it has tended to yield conclusions somewhat different from his own. Julia Kristeva has argued that the theory of polyphony is a self-defeating poetics, since it can offer no view of its own and thus loses itself in a 'polyphonic maze', where 'everything is inter-diction' ('The ruin of a poetics'). Valentina Vetlovskaya, on the other hand, does not acknowledge the existence of full-voiced polyphony in *The Brothers Karamazov*, arguing that Dostoyevsky's characters are not truly autonomous and that the reader's perceptions are manipulated by narrative authority (*Poetika romana*). Bakhtin himself conceded that 'it would be absurd to think that the author's consciousness is nowhere expressed in Dostoyevsky's novels', and he went on to explain: 'The consciousness of the creator of a polyphonic novel is constantly and everywhere present in the novel, and is active in it to the highest degree. But the function of this consciousness and the forms of its activity are different from those in the monologic novel: the author's consciousness does not transform others' consciousness (that is, the consciousnesses of the characters) into objects, and does not give them second-hand and finalising [i.e. omniscient and objective] definitions' (*Dostoevsky's Poetics*).

If this analysis is accepted and applied to *The Brothers Karamazov*, then we must marvel at the subtlety and skill with which Dostoyevsky has devised a narrative form to coincide with and confirm the dominant themes of his novel. The use of polyphony perfectly matches the disorder and diversity at the heart of the novel's thematic content, but the matter does not end there. Just as Dostoyevsky rejected Ivan's attempts in 'The Grand Inquisitor' to heal disorder and resolve contradiction by withholding freedom and forcibly absorbing discordant elements in the dictates of a higher authority, so does he refuse to employ the authority of the narrative voice to absorb and transform the dissonant voices of his characters. Instead, those voices articulating ideological positions hostile to Dostoyevsky's own are given the freedom to ensnare and subvert *themselves* through their own inner dialogue, inconsistencies, ambiguities, false notes and paradoxes. Dostoyevsky's authorial control of the work is thus asserted, but in an indirect or 'non-Euclidean' form.

In a letter to A. N. Pleshcheyev, dated 20 August 1872, Dostoyevsky commented that all his characters spoke in their own language and concepts. What is more, these voices both determine, and are determined by, the personalities of the characters to whom they belong. This may be readily illustrated in *The Brothers Karamazov*. Ivan's voice, for example, takes many forms, and these reveal the inconsistencies and paradoxes inherent in the man himself. As Terras has remarked, his dominant voice is that of radical Russian opinion in the 1860s, shaped by an unsentimental progressive rationalism neatly embodied in the two verbal leitmotifs associated with Ivan: the belief that in a world stripped of supernatural nonsense 'all is permitted', and the harrowing rejection of filial love 'Who does not desire the death of their father?' But Ivan is also a young and inexperienced man, intellectually gifted but none the less prey to a young man's emotions and sense of life, and confused by his feelings for Katerina. This aspect yields the contradictory motif of 'I love the sticky little leaves in spring', as well as the tackily sentimental confession of love for Alyosha: 'But there is one Russian boy, little Alyosha, whom I love dreadfully' (Book V, Ch. 3). Ivan's voice in its dominant rational mode may be heard most resonantly in his intellectual structures: the article on Church and State and the 'poem', 'The Grand Inquisitor'. But even in these passages Ivan's dominant voice is challenged and subverted by his other, dissonant voices. We have already considered the false notes detected by Paisy and Zosima in Ivan's article, and we should also note the adolescent reluctance and defensive embarrassment with which he presents his 'poem' to Alyosha. Terras also suggests that Ivan's dominant voice is subverted in 'The Grand Inquisitor' and elsewhere by its false and melo-dramatic rhetoric: 'That it is also an exercise in self-delusion is suggested by the masquerade and melodrama found in it: a twenty-three-year-old Russian student lets a ninety-year-old Spanish cardinal — "tall and erect" and "fiery-eyed" — express his innermost thoughts ... "The Grand Inquisitor" is not a good poem, and when everything is said and done, not very good rhetoric either' (*A Karamazov Companion*).

If the content of Ivan's speech is subverted by its empty rhetoric, then this again is entirely appropriate in the case of a character whose role in the novel is, as we have seen, to represent the destruction of life's meaning by the forms of logic. Dmitry, on the other hand, represents content seeking form, as he struggles to accommodate his overwhelming and chaotic sense of life within a moral system. Fittingly, his language is emotional, primitive, poetically charged, but formally unstructured, unsophisticated and completely bare of the calculated rhetorical devices associated with Ivan.

Indeed, at times Dmitry is quite incapable of expressing what is within him in his *own* words and can only do so by appropriating the word of others, that is to say by *quotation*. He begins his confession to Alyosha with a titanic and unsuccessful struggle for words of his own:

'Don't think I'm just chattering away out of drunkenness. I'm not drunk at all. Cognac's cognac, but I need two bottles to get drunk:
> "And Silenus, red of face
> Upon his stumbling ass ..."
... and I haven't drunk even a quarter bottle, and I'm not Silenus. I'm not Silenus [in Russian, *Silen*], but strong [in Russian, *silën* pronounced *silyon*], because I've made a final decision. Forgive the pun. You'll have to forgive me a lot today, not just a pun. Don't worry, I'm not dragging things out. I'm talking sense, and I'll get to the point in a moment. I won't beat about the bush. Wait, how does it go? ...'

He raised his head, fell into thought and suddenly and ecstatically began to recite: (Book III, Ch. 3)

Disjointed, staccato sentences and clauses, unsuccessful punning and hesitant syntax characterise this deeply felt, but ultimately unsuccessful and unformed quest for the word, until Dmitry reaches instead for Schiller's 'Ode to Joy' to shape and express the meaning of his confession.

Other characters too are disclosed through their speech. Alyosha's, for example, is characterised by a naive truthfulness completely devoid of evasion and ambiguity, as when he goes straight to the heart of Ivan's character during their long conversation: 'It's just that you're exactly the same sort of young man as all other young men of twenty-three, just as young. A young, fresh, nice, even inexperienced boy, in fact! Have I offended you terribly?' (Book V, Ch. 3). Fyodor Pavlovich's speech is built on crude linguistic play that matches his crude buffoonery, as when he plays on the various meanings of 'to love' in his defence of Grushenka before the monks: 'What is "shameful"? This "creature", this "woman of disreputable behaviour" is perhaps holier than all you soul-saving gentlemen of the monastery! Maybe she fell in her youth, a victim of her environment, but she "loved much", and Christ forgave the woman who loved much' (Book II,

Ch. 6). No translation can fully catch the mocking disrespect of 'soul-saving gentlemen' or the mock intellectualism of 'victim of her environment'. Smerdyakov's voice, too, is remarkable for the evasiveness, ambiguity, and parody of the words of others to accompany his function as a travesty. From all the foregoing it is clear that Dostoyevsky's use of the spoken word is dynamic rather than static. The speech of his characters not only passively identifies them, but also actively serves to test, and in Ivan's case to invalidate, what they stand for. This dynamism is achieved through the interaction and interplay of the novel's many voices. Sometimes a character's word is found lodged in the voice of another, as when Smerdyakov paraphrases Ivan's 'all is permitted'. When this word is deformed in its passage from one character to another, rich opportunities are opened up for implied dialogue, parody and ironic counterpoint. Such dialogue, parody and counterpoint can also arise within a single character, if an essentially unintegrated and discordant nature gives rise to conflicting voices. Ivan provides the clearest example of this: not only do we hear several voices in his case, we also experience these voices engaged in dialogue and dispute. Rozanov has pointed out that Ivan's nightmare encounter with his Devil represents 'a set of variations on "The Grand Inquisitor"' in which Ivan is confronted with, in his own words, 'everything that is stupid in my nature, everything I've long ago experienced and hammered out in my mind, everything I've cast aside like carrion' (Book XI, Ch. 9).

The Devil's voice in this episode necessarily lacks true 'otherness' since it originates in Ivan's soul and is realised through his delirious imagination. The Devil represents 'someone else's voice whispering into the ear of the hero his own words with a displaced accent' (Bakhtin, *Dostoevsky's Poetics*). He mercilessly exploits all the intellectual weaknesses, false notes, inner contradictions and empty rhetoric contained in Ivan's previous attempts to articulate his intellectual position. Yet immediately before this encounter Ivan had recognised the need to 'express his own word boldly and decisively and "to justify himself to himself"'. This is profoundly ironic,

since Ivan's 'word' as spoken by the Devil is seen to be not
his own at all. It is littered with quotations, direct and indirect,
from the whole gallery of Ivan's intellectual sources: from
Herzen, Turgenev, Belinsky, Voltaire, Schiller, Lermontov,
Gogol, Griboyedov, Descartes, Goethe, and others. The Devil's
foppish demeanour and progressive liberalism recall Turgenev;
his description of himself as 'a sort of phantom of life who
has lost all ends and beginnings' obliquely refers to the title
of Herzen's essay of 1862–3, 'Ends and Beginnings'; his
assertion that 'Je pense, donc je suis' directly quotes Descartes's
well-known aphorism; and so on. The many examples of
such quotations are carefully analysed in Perlina, *Varieties of
Poetic Utterance*. In this way Ivan's 'originality' is brought
into question; his word is shown, to both the reader and himself,
to be secondhand rhetoric, the borrowed word of others. In
this way the Devil's voice fails to justify Ivan to himself.
Instead of reinforcing Ivan's ideas, it embarrasses him by
revealing his own lack of originality and naivety. At one point
Ivan, 'blushing all over with shame', forbids the Devil to
mention 'The Grand Inquisitor'. This in itself is significant,
for earlier Ivan had told his visitor: 'You are I, I myself, only
with a different mug. You can only say what I am thinking; it
is not in your power to say anything new to me' (Book XI,
Ch. 9). But if the Devil cannot surprise Ivan with the content
of his speech, he certainly can with its form. As Bakhtin
explains, 'Ivan's words and the Devil's replies do not differ
in content but only in tone, only in accent. But this change
of accent changes their entire ultimate meaning'. This formal
rearrangement ultimately constitutes a 'new word', since it
invests the serious with irony and ambiguity, and thereby
subjects what Ivan holds dear to ridicule and travesty.

Terras has carefully traced in Ivan's nightmare a detailed
and progressive parody of 'The Grand Inquisitor', and con-
sequently illustration here may be confined to a single example.
Towards the end of their encounter the Devil presents a highly
subversive recapitulation of what is clearly one of Ivan's
earlier versions of 'The Grand Inquisitor', a project entitled
'The Geological Upheaval'. This compares in importance the

moment in human history when man proclaims his independence from God with the onset of a new age in the earth's geological evolution. At that moment 'people will unite to seize from life all that it has to offer, but inevitably for the sake of happiness and joy in this world alone.' Man will then become the 'man-God', uninhibited by superstition, freed from the yoke of religion, and confident in his own moral independence. We recognise here both the age-old dream of rational, atheistic humanism and the particular inflection Ivan has given to this ideal in 'The Grand Inquisitor'. But the Devil's voice continues:

In this sense 'all is permitted' to man. What is more, even if this period never comes to pass, then since there is still no God and no immortality, it follows that the new man is permitted to become the man-god, even though he may be the only one in the whole world, and of course in this new role he may with impunity leap over every moral barrier that constrained the previous slave-man, if he so wishes. There is no law for a god! Where a god stands, that is his place. Wherever I stand will become the starting point — 'all is permitted' and that's all there is to it! All this is very nice; only, if you want to behave like a scoundrel why bother with the sanction of truth? But that's our modern Russian man for you: he won't be a scoundrel unless he has the sanction of truth. That's how much the truth has come to mean for him ...   (Book XI, Ch. 9)

In this cynical argument, where moral freedom is reduced to the right to behave like a scoundrel, the highflown humanist rhetoric of 'The Grand Inquisitor' is shown for what it really is: a shabby and hypocritical recipe for criminal self-indulgence. At this moment in Ivan's mind his own responsibility for the murder of his father becomes apparent, and the impressive image of the rebellious Inquisitor must be replaced by the hideous face of the slippery parricide, Smerdyakov.

Dostoyevsky's use of polyphony in passages such as this invested his treatment of ideas and his presentation of character with a relativistic and 'unfinalised' quality which, as Bakhtin argued, marked a new stage in the development of the realistic novel. Indeed, many critics have argued that this same unfinalised quality is to be found in the novel as a whole. In his author's preface Dostoyevsky suggested that he had in mind not one novel, but two, the first corresponding to the extant text of *The Brothers Karamazov* and the other dealing with Alyosha's life up to the 'present moment'. These remarks have encouraged among some critics the belief that Dostoyevsky's grand design for his final novel was interrupted by his death and that the surviving text represents only a half-realised fragment. Attempts have even been made to reconstruct Dostoyevsky's plans for the unwritten 'continuation', even though the writer himself showed little evidence of work on such a project between the completion of the existing novel and his death two months later (see, for example, Belov, 'Eshchyo odna versiya'). All such speculation belongs, in any case, to the realm of literary history rather than literary analysis, and the text of *The Brothers Karamazov* represents, as it stands, both a perfect form for the expression of Dostoyevsky's discordant vision and the very pinnacle of his achievement as a novelist.

Chapter 3

The critical reception

The Brothers Karamazov, like most other novels of its time,
appeared in serial form in the periodical press before it was sold
as a separate volume. It was published in sixteen instalments
in *The Russian Herald* between January 1879 and November
1880, and it evoked widespread interest: 'They are reading
the novel everywhere and writing me letters. The young are
reading it, high society is reading it, the literary world is either
abusing me or praising me. Never before, in terms of creating
an impression, have I enjoyed such success', Dostoyevsky wrote
in December 1879 (XXX/1, 132). He was by now confident of
his high standing in the eyes of the Russian reading public,
but he fully expected the outrage of professional reviewers
from the progressive intelligentsia. The fact that the first
reviews of the novel appeared while it was still being written
meant that they were necessarily of a provisional nature and,
more intriguingly, that they possibly helped to shape Dostoyevsky's conception of the later parts of his work (Todd, '*The
Brothers Karamazov* and the poetics'). The novel appeared
at a critical moment in Russian history, and this fact too,
determined how it was received. Its publication coincided with
an uneasy truce among usually hostile factions of the Russian
intelligentsia, a truce occasioned by the Pushkin celebrations
of June 1880 and especially by Dostoyevsky's own Pushkin
speech, which had been hailed as a great moral event and a
turning point in Russian intellectual life. However, shortly
after Dostoyevsky's death this fragile truce was shattered by
the assassination of Alexander II and the opening up of new
rifts among conservative, moderate and radical social opinion
that were to continue until 1917.

Already by the end of 1879 over thirty reviews of the novel
had appeared in the St Petersburg press, with many more

published in provincial newspapers and journals (see XV,
487ff.). There was widespread, if not quite unanimous, agreement among critics of all political persuasions that the novel
marked the summit of Dostoyevsky's artistic achievement and a
significant moment in the history of Russian literature. Critical
disagreement emerged, quite understandably, from consideration of the novel's philosophical content. Radical criticism
focused on Dostoyevsky's obscurantism and advocacy of a
reactionary, 'mystical' outlook. One critic, in the journal *Golos*
(Voice), complained about the author's unfair treatment of progressive thinkers: 'There is not a single "developed" man who
is not a scoundrel, or a psychiatric case, or about to subvert
honour and justice' (XV, 488). Conversely, the novel's positive
heroes were confined to those who wore cassocks. Others took
issue with what they saw as Dostoyevsky's naive Christian
utopianism: 'Mr Dostoyevsky is frankly convinced that as soon
as his pious ideas are put into effect, brotherly love will reign
on earth, filled with humility and universal forgiveness. Unfor-
tunately history demonstrates that life is not like that' (XV,
488). This belief that life was not as shown in *The Brothers
Karamazov* became a leitmotif of radical criticism of the novel,
and Dostoyevsky was accused of ignoring social reality in favour
of 'a truth that is Mr Dostoyevsky's own, characterised by
gloomy, mystical fanaticism and outbursts almost of madness'
(XV, 489). The most significant example of such criticism was
M. A. Antonovich's essay, 'A Mystical-ascetic Novel', which
appeared in *Novoye obozreniye* (New Review) in 1881. Antonovich had earlier succeeded Chernyshevsky and Dobrolyubov
in the reviews section of *The Contemporary*, and his aesthetic
views were distinguished by the same utilitarianism and aver-
sion to the notion of 'pure art'. His opinion of *The Brothers
Karamazov* was that it was not a novel, 'but some sort of
medieval tract on how to save your soul'. Its message of religious
self-improvement was unnatural, retrograde, anti-humanist
and entirely out of keeping with the spirit of the age.

Ironically, Dostoyevsky was also accused of departing from
the norms of Orthodox Christianity and of sharing the democratic humanism espoused by his radical opponents. In August

1880 he received from Pobedonostsev a copy of Konstantin Leontyev's article 'On Universal Love', in which Leontyev argued that Dostoyevsky's advocacy of universal brotherhood in both *The Brothers Karamazov* and his Pushkin speech smacked of heretical utopianism by suggesting the possibility of paradise on earth, a proposition not acknowledged in Leontyev's interpretation of Orthodox doctrine. This suggestion, that Dostoyevsky himself suffered from what Leontyev called '*mania democratica progressiva*', almost certainly arose because Leontyev, like so many critics after him, made the fundamental error of confusing Dostoyevsky's voice with those of his characters.

Nikolay Mikhaylovsky's famous essay of 1882, 'A Cruel Talent', dismissed altogether the idea that Dostoyevsky might be a progressive humanist. Instead, it argued that the behaviour of Dostoyevsky's characters was 'causeless' in that it was derived solely from the author's own perverse whims and taste for cruelty. Mikhaylovsky attempted to demonstrate that in the course of Dostoyevsky's career his heroes changed from being predominantly 'sheep' (i.e. the downtrodden) into 'wolves' (i.e. the rapacious exploiters of others), and that in his last works he delighted in the gratuitous and aimless torture of the sheep by the wolves. This view was shared by the novelist Ivan Turgenev, who had particular reason to hate Dostoyevsky for an unflattering caricature in *The Devils* and who regarded him as a particularly nasty specimen, a Russian Marquis de Sade. Tolstoy too voiced similar doubts. In 1883 he confessed to being unable to finish *The Brothers Karamazov*, although he later came to admire the work and especially 'A Russian Monk', finding the ideals expressed in it close to his own (XV, 511–12). The writer Maxim Gorky, who met Tolstoy on several occasions towards the end of the latter's life, has left a memoir of these meetings, in which he records that when Tolstoy spoke of Dostoyevsky he did so 'unwillingly and with great effort, as if trying to avoid or overcome something'. 'He felt much, but he thought badly', Tolstoy confided, speaking of Dostoyevsky. 'He was mistrustful, vain, difficult and unhappy. It is strange that he is so widely read. I cannot understand why. It is all so

heavy and useless, since all these Idiots, Raw Youths, Raskol-
nikovs and so on are not at all real. In reality everything is
simpler and easier to understand'. Tolstoy also touched upon
Dostoyevsky's perversity, claiming that he lacked the courage
to make his characters healthy: 'He was convinced that since
he was sick, the whole world was sick with him'. Gorky himself subscribed to, and helped to popularise, this view of
Dostoyevsky as a sick and perverse talent. In an article of
1913 he described him as 'our evil genius' and coined the term
'Karamazovism' to describe the human bestiality with which
the author was besotted and which did nothing to improve
man's social condition.

Dostoyevsky's 'mysticism' and apparent 'perversity' were,
however, received more positively by the conservative and less
socially engaged sections of the Russian intelligentsia. V. V.
Rozanov's analysis of 'The Grand Inquisitor', which appeared
in 1890, was the first sustained and reasonably objective account
of Dostoyevsky's belief in man's essentially irrational and
mystical nature which (according to Rozanov) could find true
freedom only in religion. D. S. Merezhkovsky's famous study
(1902) contrasted Dostoyevsky with Tolstoy, arguing that
whereas the latter was a pagan and sensual writer preoccupied
exclusively with the physical world, Dostoyevsky was the 'seer'
of a transcendental spiritual world, whose works were prophetic
and revelatory in that they penetrated 'the illusoriness of the
real'. S. N. Bulgakov, in an essay of 1902, saw Ivan Karamazov
as a nineteenth-century Russian Faust whose philosophical
idealism soared beyond the transient to the eternal, an approach
further developed in Lev Shestov's study of Dostoyevsky and
Nietzsche, published the following year. Perhaps the most
significant example of this type of criticism was Vyacheslav
Ivanov's innovative study of Dostoyevsky and the 'novel-
tragedy'. First published in 1911, it has appeared in English
translation under the title *Freedom and the Tragic Life*. Ivanov
was the first to recognise the importance of myth in Dostoyevsky's novels and the first to analyse the author's use of formal
dramatic devices. His study anticipated the work of Bakhtin
by showing that the novels of Dostoyevsky broke new ground

in their use of catastrophe to explore the tragic nature of their heroes, in their emphasis on speech, gesture and the set scene, and in their reliance upon counterpoint and polyphony. This approach did much to offset the almost exclusive concentration of earlier criticism on the philosophical and ideological content of Dostoyevsky's novels, and it prepared the ground for the eventual reappraisal of the view that Dostoyevsky lacked formal sense and craftsmanship.

In the meantime, Dostoyevsky's reputation had spread to the West, often on the basis of quite inadequate translations. Melchior de Vogüé's *Le roman Russe* (1886) served to introduce the European reading public to the achievements of the Russian novel, although his opinion was that Dostoyevsky was a lesser talent than either Tolstoy or Turgenev. Like others before him, de Vogüé scented something elemental and unsavoury in Dostoyevsky, referring to him as 'le vrai Scythe', a barbarian at the door. He did, however, recognise the tragic roots of Dostoyevsky's art, and conceded that he had the power to change his readers' 'habitudes intellectuelles' through his concern with the depths of human suffering and the religious force of his novels. De Vogüé was also amongst the first to recognise that Dostoyevsky's intense and discordant vision aligned him with the Romantic tradition and such writers as E. T. A. Hoffmann, Poe and Baudelaire. Early English criticism was generally negative. Indeed, the first full-length article in English on Dostoyevsky, John Lomas's 'Dostoïewsky and His Work' (*MacMillan's Magazine* 55 (1887)), suggested that his work after *Crime and Punishment* 'ceased to have any special value'. The sticking point for many English critics was, once again, the perverse, exaggerated and implausible nature of Dostoyevsky's realism. *The Spectator*, reviewing *The Idiot* in 1887, remarked that 'the so-called realism which consists in a display of deformities, more or less hideous, dragged forth and paraded for the public to gloat over...is unquestionably unattractive'. This view only began to change after the publication in 1912 of Constance Garnett's fine translation of *The Brothers Karamazov* and the appearance in the same year of the first English book-length study, J. A. T. Lloyd's biography *A Great*

Russian Realist: Feodor Dostoieffsky. These publications prepared the way for the development of an extravagant 'cult of Dostoyevsky' amongst English intellectuals, the most sensational example of which was John Middleton Murry's book *Fyodor Dostoevsky: A Critical Study* (1916). Murry's enthusiastic analysis of Dostoyevsky as a demonic prophet whose novels represented visionary outpourings of 'metaphysical obscenity' was counterbalanced by D.H. Lawrence's clear distaste for Dostoyevsky's excesses and religious extravagances: he referred to him in 1915 as 'like the rat, slithering along in hate, in the shadows, and in order to belong to the light, professing love, all love ... He is not nice'. The following year he wrote to Murry, in response to the latter's book: 'Dostoievsky... can nicely stick his head between the feet of Christ, and waggle his behind in the air. And though the behind-wagglings are a revelation, I don't think much even of the feet of Christ as a bluff for the cowards to hide their eyes against'. Lawrence also wrote a piece specifically on 'The Grand Inquisitor' (1930), in which he too confused Dostoyevsky's voice with that of one of his characters: '[Ivan] is also, of course, Dostoyevsky himself... We cannot doubt that the Inquisitor speaks Dostoyevsky's own final opinion about Jesus'. This failure to recognise the dispersal of the author's voice meant that, while Lawrence noted and disapproved of the 'showing off' and 'cynical-satanical pose' of the legend, he did not see that these were also part of a sustained authorial design calculated to discredit Ivan and what he stands for.

A similar misunderstanding of Dostoyevsky's relationship to the characters he created informed Sigmund Freud's famous essay, 'Dostoyevsky and Parricide', first published in 1928. Freud argued that Dostoyevsky's tendency to depict neurotic types disclosed deep-seated sado-masochistic traits in his own nature, which could be traced back to the trauma of his father's death (of the circumstances of which Freud was as ignorant as other critics). The key to understanding *The Brothers Karamazov* thus lay in the novel's oblique exploration of Oedipal and homosexual complexes. Freud's essay, notwithstanding its eccentricity, serves to illustrate the extent to which

Dostoyevsky's art had been absorbed into the European intellectual, as opposed to merely literary, tradition by the 1920s. Hermann Hesse had written on *The Brothers Karamazov* in 1923 in a way that made it clear that he saw the novel as not just a work of art, but a pointer to the European cultural collapse. Albert Einstein had discerned in Dostoyevsky's work 'the emotional, psychological and aesthetic equivalent' of his own physical theories (Kuznetsov 1972), and claimed that Dostoyevsky had given him more than any other thinker. André Gide (1923) had explored Dostoyevsky as a psychologist and philosopher of human freedom in a study that did much to pave the way for Dostoyevsky's later 'adoption' by the French Existentialists, particularly J.-P. Sartre and Albert Camus. Camus's work of 1951, *L'Homme révolté*, is centred on a discussion of Ivan Karamazov's revolt, and such clear indebtedness has seen Dostoyevsky claimed by some as the father of modern Existentialist thought, a claim which overlooks his advocacy of an essentially Christian world outlook. Further, a heavily stressed Russian text of *The Brothers Karamazov* was one of the very few books owned by Ludwig Wittgenstein.

In Russia, Dostoyevsky's standing as a 'classic' of Russian literature, comparable in stature to Tolstoy, came under scrutiny after the Revolution of October 1917, as a new generation of Marxist critics addressed themselves to the task of re-examining the literature of the imperial past in the light of the ideological requirements of the new socialist regime. The problems that were to confront Soviet Dostoyevsky scholars had already been identified by earlier Russian critics of the novelist. On the one hand there was enough in Dostoyevsky's work to support the view that his novels represented a clear indictment of a corrupt and disintegrating Tsarist reality, and a call for a new social order based on human brotherhood and equality. On the other hand, it was equally clear that Dostoyevsky's concept of brotherhood had little to do with the socialist ideals espoused by the Bolsheviks. It turned instead on the sort of reactionary, mystical chauvinism that had been identified in his work by Antonovich and Gorky, and which was clearly incompatible with the militant atheism of the Soviet state. Could Dostoyevsky and his work be accommodated in that brave new world, or was he to be abandoned in the ruins of the bourgeois order? Could his work be pressed into the service of revolution, or did it present a dangerous moral and ideological challenge to the ideals of the new regime? Such questions certainly arose in the immediately post-revolutionary years, but the starkness of the choice they offered was largely obscured by the atmosphere of toleration, experimentation and diversity that prevailed in the early 1920s. Soviet scholarship was mostly left alone to debate Dostoyevsky's ideological strengths and weaknesses, to explore and collate the mass of documentary material newly uncovered in the archives, and even to undertake the sustained effort to define and analyse his stylistics that culminated in the work of Bakhtin.

The end of the 1920s, however, saw the rise of Stalin to supreme power, the gradual end of the spirited artistic debates of the first decade of the Revolution, and the victory of a narrowly ideological and hostile view of Dostoyevsky, as Soviet society and intellectual life settled into the drab conformity and strict Party orthodoxy of the 1930s. Dostoyevsky was now unambiguously a dangerous writer – both for Soviet society and for those critics who still tried to find a niche for him in the pantheon of Russian classics. Although he was never an 'unperson', publication of his works was erratic and, with few exceptions, little effort was made by Soviet critics to rise to the moral, philosophical and aesthetic challenges offered by his art. Instead his novels were mined for anti-capitalist sentiments, sympathy for the oppressed classes, and – during World War Two – anti-German prejudice. Since the Khrushchev thaw, Soviet Dostoyevsky criticism has gradually recovered the sophistication it displayed in the 1920s and, when combined with the immense interest that continues to be shown in his work in the West, it forms one of the largest bodies of critical literature ever devoted to a single author.

The influence of Dostoyevsky on the subsequent development of world literature has been immense. Indeed, it is arguable that *The Brothers Karamazov* has contributed more to the content and shape of modern fiction than any other single novel, and this renders full analysis of this influence quite impossible in a study of this size. The central themes of the novel – its concern with human alienation and exposure of the inadequacy of reason, its depiction of a fragmented, unstable world, and its attempts to rediscover a core of permanent values – have all become the common currency of twentieth-century fiction. Even more striking is the extent to which later writers have absorbed Dostoyevsky's *artistic* example, implicitly quoting passages from his fiction and weaving his technical innovations into new literary contexts. In Russia the publication of *The Brothers Karamazov* marked both the culminating point of the Russian realistic novel and the beginning of its decline. The fact that Dostoyevsky had combined his depiction of the social order with mythical and symbolic dimensions helped as much as anything to encourage the Modernist movement of the 1880s and 1890s, with its concentration on the 'more real' of the aesthetic and the mystical and its neglect of the 'real', which had been the province of the social novel. In Soviet literature Dostoyevsky's general influence is clearly seen in the psychological novels of Leonid Leonov, but a more specific and deliberate dialogue with *The Brothers Karamazov* is set up in Yevgeny Zamyatin's anti-utopian novel *We* (1920), where the Grand Inquisitor's ideal of a few enlightened individuals guarding the secret and imposing a mathematical happiness and equality on the sheeplike multitude is translated into the forms of twentieth-century political totalitarianism. (Incidentally, through Zamyatin Dostoyevsky certainly contributed to the conception of George Orwell's nightmare *1984*.) More recently, the novels of Alexander Solzhenitsyn make the same use of polyphony and emphasis on the primacy of the subjective voice that distinguished Dostoyevsky's art, although the essentially stable moral certainties to be found in the enclosed worlds of *One Day in the Life of Ivan Denisovich, Cancer Ward* and *The First Circle* are far removed from Dostoyevsky's discordant vision of moral relativism.

In English literature Robert Louis Stevenson was the first writer to betray in his work the effects of reading Dostoyevsky.

To be sure, his admiration for the Russian novelist was focused on *Crime and Punishment*, of which Stevenson's novel *Markheim* is practically an imitation. But Stevenson showed that he had absorbed some of the more general characteristics of Dostoyevsky's art, including its intensity, its psychological complexity and the techniques used to convey feverish and hallucinatory states of mind. Joseph Conrad's *Under Western Eyes* was a deliberate attempt to 'capture the soul of things Russian' at a time when Russian literature was very much in vogue in Europe. Conrad disliked Dostoyevsky, and some of the scenes of misery and darkness in this novel seem like deliberate pastiche of Dostoyevskian gloom. But his literary relationship with Dostoyevsky was complex, and some aspects of his work, such as his depiction of corruption, evil and moral anxiety and his use of character doubling (in, for example, *Heart of Darkness* and *Lord Jim*), suggest that his distaste provided no immunity from Dostoyevsky's art. The same is probably true of Lawrence, who disliked what he considered to be Dostoyevsky's moral posturing, but who might well have borrowed the latter's provisional and fluid approach to plot and characterisation for works like the short novel *The Trespasser* (1912), and who certainly drew heavily upon 'The Grand Inquisitor' for his tale of the Resurrection 'The Man Who Died' (1931).

Dostoyevsky's retreat from the narrative objectivity associated with the social novel found an influential counterpart in Marcel Proust's *A la recherche du temps perdu*, a sustained meditation in which the narrator's portrait of society is deliberately contaminated with filaments of his mood, memories, desires and tastes. Interestingly, Proust – who found Dostoyevsky largely alien to his tastes – did comment positively on the Russian novelist's genius for narrative construction. The 'stream-of-consciousness' form of James Joyce's *Ulysses* betrays a similar lack of trust in narrative objectivity and a thoroughly Dostoyevskian attempt to allow the reader direct access to the consciousness of the fictional characters, apparently unmodified by narrative authority.

Dostoyevsky's art, and *The Brothers Karamazov* in particular, resonate in the work of several of the most significant German novelists of the twentieth century. Thomas Mann's article 'Dostoyevsky − in Moderation', first published in 1945, acknowledged Dostoyevsky's greatness, but questioned his 'unhealthy' preoccupation with the morbid, demonic and pathological. Despite this, Mann conceded that in his work on *Doctor Faustus* he had drawn upon Dostoyevsky's 'sick, apocalyptic-grotesque world'. This is particularly evident in chapter 25 of *Doctor Faustus*, where the example of Ivan Karamazov's nightmare allowed Mann to solve the problem of inserting the traditional German motif of a pact with the devil into the framework of a modern realistic novel. Dostoyevsky's approach had been to strip Ivan's devil of all supernatural trappings and present him as a prosaic social sponger, and to scale down the religious struggle between Good and Evil into the psychological dualism of bickering voices within Ivan's hallucination. The demeanour and appearance of Adrian Leverkühn's 'visitor', with his indecently tight breeches, worn yellow shoes and vigorous attempts to persuade Adrian of his 'reality', are a clear acknowledgement of Dostoyevsky's influence. Like Mann, Hermann Hesse addressed directly the question of what Dostoyevsky meant to him in a series of essays written between 1915 and 1925, one of which was specifically devoted to the 'novel-myth', *The Brothers Karamazov*. From these Dostoyevsky emerged as a prophet of the chaos enveloping Europe after the First World War. In *Steppenwolf*, a densely symbolic novel, Hesse followed Dostoyevsky in depicting a tragically alienated intellectual in a dualistic universe. Hesse's hero, significantly, has on his bookshelf a few heavily annotated volumes of Dostoyevsky's works. Franz Kafka also extended Dostoyevsky's depiction of an unstable, chaotic world in which the alienation of contemporary *homo absurdus* is complete. Kafka read *The Brothers Karamazov* in two German translations, and his *The Trial* shows clear thematic affinities with Dostoyevsky's novel in its treatment of law, punishment and the courtroom. It also betrays Kafka's reading of Dostoyevsky's descriptive prose in its account of dark, airless corridors, squalid courtyards, and the dislocation of the characters' gestures from their mental states. But the characters that in Dostoyevsky's novels are required both to embody contemporary myth and ideas *and* to act out convincing social and psychological roles are reduced in the work of Kafka to schematic cyphers, abstract symbols of man's hopelessness in the face of blind necessity. The situations, too — the arrest and the subsequent trial — are anonymous and invested with an absolute, impersonal quality. In *The Brothers Karamazov*, despite its espousal of myth and symbolism, we are still in the world of the nineteenth-century realistic novel; in Kafka the action is unanchored and the characters detached from any recognisable depiction of the 'real' world.

Any full treatment of Dostoyevsky's literary influence would include discussion of William Faulkner, Theodore Dreiser, Thomas Wolfe, Graham Greene, Iris Murdoch, Heinrich Böll, Max Frisch, the 'magical realism' of contemporary Latin-American novelists, and much more. The few examples considered here can only suggest the nature and extent of Dostoyevsky's impact on modern fiction as it evolved from the nineteenth-century social novel, with its pretensions to realism and narrative objectivity, towards the *nouveau roman*, where the objects of perception and the act of perception are inextricably interwoven in a celebration of subjectivity.

... All the cries of the critics to the effect that I do not depict real life have not disenchanted me. There are no bases to our society ... One colossal quake and the whole lot will come to an end, collapse, and be negated as though it had never existed. And this is not just outwardly true, as in the West, but inwardly, morally so. Our talented writers, people like Tolstoy and Goncharov, who with great artistry depict family life in upper-middle-class circles, think that they are depicting the life of the majority. In my view they have depicted only the life of the exceptions, but the life which I portray is the life that is the general rule. Future generations, more objective in their view, will see that this is so. The truth is on my side, I am convinced of that. I am proud that I was the first to portray the real man *of the Russian majority* and the first to reveal his abnormal and tragic aspect. Tragedy consists in consciousness of abnormality ... I alone have depicted the tragedy of the underground, which consists in suffering, self-punishment, and in consciousness of the existence of something better alongside the impossibility of achieving it ...   (XVI, 329)

This passage, dated 22 March 1875, is from Dostoyevsky's preparatory notebooks for *A Raw Youth*. In it he comes as close as he ever did to defining what he felt to be the meaning of his artistic achievement and to anticipating the enduring significance of this achievement for generations, and no doubt centuries, to come. *The Brothers Karamazov* cemented this achievement, and few would now dispute Dostoyevsky's claim upon the hearts and minds of future generations, although many would disagree with his apparent allocation of secondary status to Tolstoy. George Steiner, while recognising the latter's clear claims to greatness and immortality, does, however, conclude that 'Dostoyevsky has penetrated more deeply than Tolstoy into the fabric of contemporary thought' and has contributed more than any other writer of the nineteenth century towards determining the 'shape and psychology' of twentieth-century fiction (*Tolstoy or Dostoevsky*). A similar claim is made by Alex de Jonge when he suggests that, along with Marcel Proust, Dostoyevsky is the artist most 'supremely representative' of the modern age (*Dostoevsky and the Age*). Dostoyevsky has refused to settle into the role of venerable 'classic'. His works, and particularly *The Brothers Karamazov*, still retain, more than a century on, both an enduring fascination and a remarkable sense of contemporary relevance. As Dostoyevsky himself predicted, Tolstoy's novels, with their epic calm and affirmation of normality in the ebb and flow of existence, now evoke an age and a temper long since passed. Dostoyevsky's works, however, with their disturbing insights into ideological pluralism, social and moral disintegration, perverse psychology, rebellion, criminality and spiritual anxiety, still appear strikingly immediate and revelatory.

The key to Dostoyevsky's enduring contemporary appeal is suggested in the notebook extracts cited above and is fully revealed in *The Brothers Karamazov*. First, his work discloses the provisional and unstable nature of contemporary existence, which has lost both the spiritual certainty and the faith in the power of reason which sustained man in earlier ages. Secondly, he depicts the tragic and 'abnormal' nature of modern man, who is condemned by his lack of faith to amoralism and the desert of existential uncertainty, anxiety and doubt. Thirdly, he has recognised that man's sense of spiritual isolation is accompanied, and indeed sharpened, by a longing for new certainties to replace those that have been lost. The collapse of confidence in rational science and material progress among large sections of the developed world in the twentieth century, along with the cultivation of new, 'alternative' roads to enlightenment, perfectly confirm Dostoyevsky's diagnosis. Finally, in Dostoyevsky's polyphonic depiction of philosophical pluralism the contemporary reader recognises a reflection of the profound discords that disturb the modern world. More than a hundred years after its publication, *The Brothers Karamazov* continues to offer us insight into the moral, social, political, psychological and spiritual crises that afflict our culture. It was Dostoyevsky's deepest hope that it also indicated the way to overcome them.

Guide to further reading

This guide is limited to works cited or found useful in the preparation of this study. It consists for the most part of book-length critical studies; articles are mentioned only when they have been specifically quoted. A bibliographical section is provided for those wishing to explore more fully the vast literature on Dostoyevsky and *The Brothers Karamazov*.

Edition of Dostoyevsky's works in Russian

Polnoye sobraniye sochineniy v tridtsati tomakh (Nauka edition), Moscow, 1972 onwards (publication still in progress).

Translations of relevant works by Dostoyevsky

The Brothers Karamazov translated by Constance Garnett, London, 1912 and many subsequent editions.

The Brothers Karamazov translated by D. Magarshack, Harmondsworth, 1958 and many subsequent editions.

Fyodor Dostoevsky: The Notebooks for 'The Brothers Karamazov' edited and translated by E. Wasiolek, Chicago and London, 1971.

The Unpublished Dostoevsky: Diaries and Notebooks, 1860–1881 edited and translated by C. Proffer in 3 vols., Ann Arbor, Mich., 1973–6.

The Diary of a Writer translated by B. Brasol, Santa Barbara and Salt Lake City, 1979.

Other sources used

N. Fyodorov, *Sochineniya*, Moscow, 1982.

Russian Philosophy edited and translated in 3 vols., by J. M. Edie, J. P. Scanlan, M. B. Zeldin and G. L. Kline, Chicago, 1965.

Bibliographies

[Gosudarstvennyy literaturnyy muzey F. M. Dostoyevskogo], *F. M. Dostoyevsky: Bibliografiya proizvedeniy F. M. Dostoyevskogo i literatury o nyom, 1917–1965*, Moscow, 1968. Supplements in *Dostoyevsky i ego vremya* ed. V. G. Bazanov and G. M. Fridlender, Moscow, 1971 and *Dostoyevsky: Materialy i issledovaniya* ed. G. M. Fridlender, Leningrad, 1974.

W. J. Leatherbarrow, *Fedor Dostoevsky: A Reference Guide*, Boston, Mass., 1990.
There is also a useful guide to works on *The Brothers Karamazov* in V. Terras, *A Karamazov Companion* (see below).

Works of historical interest cited in chapter 3

Antonovich, M. A., 'Mistiko-asketicheskiy roman: *Brat'ya Karamazovy*'. In *Izbrannye stat'i*, Leningrad, 1938.
Bulgakov, S. N., 'Ivan Karamazov kak filosofskiy tip'. In *Ot marksizma k idealizmu*, St Petersburg, 1903.
Camus, Albert, *L'Homme révolté*, Paris, 1951.
De Vogüé, M., *Le roman Russe*, Paris, 1886.
Freud, Sigmund, 'Dostoevsky and Parricide'. In *Dostoevsky: A Collection of Critical Essays*, ed. R. Wellek, Englewood Cliffs, N. J., 1962.
Gide, André, *Dostoievsky: Articles et causeries*, Paris, 1923.
Gorky, M., 'O Karamazovshchine'. In *Sobraniye sochineniy* (30 vols.), Moscow, 1949–56, Vol. 24, pp. 146–57.
  On Tolstoy, Letchworth, 1966.
Ivanov, Vyacheslav, *Freedom and the Tragic Life: A Study in Dostoevsky*, translated by N. Cameron, London, 1952.
Lawrence, D. H., 'Preface to Dostoevsky's *The Grand Inquisitor*'. In *Dostoevsky: A Collection of Critical Essays*, ed. R. Wellek.
Leontyev, K. N., 'O vsemirnoy lyubvi: Rech' Dostoyevskogo na Pushkinskom prazdnike'. In *Dostoyevsky i Pushkin*, ed. A. L. Flekser, St Petersburg, 1921.
Merezhkovsky, D. S., *Tolstoi as Man and Artist, with an Essay on Dostoievski*, New York, 1902.
Mikhaylovsky, N., *A Cruel Talent*, translated by S. Cadmus, Ann Arbor, Mich., 1978.
Murry, John Middleton, *Fyodor Dostoevsky: A Critical Study*, London, 1916.
Rozanov, V.V., *Dostoevsky and the Legend of the Grand Inquisitor*, translated by S. E. Roberts, Ithaca, 1972.
Shestov, Lev, *Dostoevsky, Tolstoy and Nietzsche*, translated by S. E. Roberts, Athens, Ohio, 1969.

Biographical and critical works

Bakhtin, M. M., *Problems of Dostoevsky's Poetics*, translated by C. Emerson, Manchester, 1984.
Belknap, R., *The Genesis of The Brothers Karamazov: The Aesthetics, Ideology, and Psychology of Making a Text*, Evanston, Illinois, 1990.
  The Structure of The Brothers Karamazov, The Hague and Paris, 1967.

Belov, S., 'Eshchyo odna versiya o prodolzhenii *Brat'ev Karama-zovykh'*, *Voprosy literatury*, 1971, no. 10, pp. 254–5.

Catteau, J., *Dostoyevsky and the Process of Literary Creation*, translated by A. Littlewood, Cambridge, 1989.

Čiževskyj, D., 'Schiller und die *Brüder Karamazov'*, *Zeitschrift für slavische Philologie*, 6 (1929), pp. 1–42.

de Jonge, A., *Dostoevsky and the Age of Intensity*, London, 1975.

Dolinin, A. S., *Posledniye romany Dostoyevskogo: Kak sozdavalis' 'Podrostok' i 'Brat'ya Karamazovy'*, Moscow and Leningrad, 1963.

Dowler, W., *Dostoevsky, Grigor'ev, and Native Soil Conservatism*, Toronto, 1982.

Dunlop, J. B., *Staretz Amvrosy: Model for Dostoevsky's Staretz Zossima*, Belmont, Mass., 1972.

Fanger, D., *Dostoevsky and Romantic Realism: A Study of Dostoevsky in Relation to Balzac, Dickens and Gogol*, Cambridge, Mass., 1965.

Frank, J., *Dostoevsky: The Seeds of Revolt, 1821–1849*, Princeton, 1976.
  Dostoevsky: The Years of Ordeal, 1850–1859, Princeton, 1983.
  Dostoevsky: The Stir of Liberation, 1860–1865, Princeton, 1986.

Gibson, A. Boyce, *The Religion of Dostoevsky*, London, 1973.

Grossman, L., *Dostoevsky*, translated by M. Mackler, London, 1974.

Hackel, S., 'The religious dimension: vision or evasion? Zosima's discourse in *The Brothers Karamazov'*. In *New Essays on Dostoevsky*, ed. M. V. Jones and G. M. Terry, Cambridge, 1983.

Hingley, R., *The Undiscovered Dostoyevsky*, London, 1962.

Holquist, J. M., *Dostoevsky and the Novel*, Princeton, 1977.

Jackson, R. L., *The Art of Dostoevsky: Deliriums and Nocturnes*, Princeton, 1981.
  Dostoevsky's Quest for Form: A Study of his Philosophy of Art, New Haven, 1966.

Jones, J., *Dostoevsky*, Oxford, 1983.

Jones, M. V., *Dostoyevsky after Bakhtin*, Cambridge, 1990.
  Dostoyevsky: The Novel of Discord, London, 1976.

Kjetsaa, G., *Fyodor Dostoyevsky: A Writer's Life*, London, 1988.

Kristeva, J., 'The ruin of a poetics'. In *Russian Formalism*, ed. S. Bann and J. E. Bowlt, Edinburgh, 1983.

Kuznetsov, B., *Einstein and Dostoyevsky*, translated by V. Talmy, London, 1972.

Lampert, E., 'Dostoevsky'. In *Nineteenth Century Russian Literature*, ed. J. Fennell, London, 1973.

Leatherbarrow, W. J., *Fedor Dostoevsky*, Boston, Mass., 1981.

Linnér, S., *Dostoevskij on Realism*, Stockholm, 1967.
  Starets Zosima in 'The Brothers Karamazov': A Study in the Mimesis of Virtue, Stockholm, 1975.

Lord, R., *Dostoevsky: Essays and Perspectives*, London, 1970.

Matlaw, R., *The Brothers Karamazov: Novelistic Technique*, The Hague, 1957.

Mirsky, D. S., *A History of Russian Literature*, London, 1949.

Mochulsky, K., *Dostoevsky: His Life and Work*, translated by M. Minihan, Princeton, 1967.

Morson, G. S., *The Boundaries of Genre: Dostoevsky's Diary of a Writer and the Traditions of Literary Utopia*, Austin, Texas, 1981.

'Verbal pollution in *The Brothers Karamazov*'. In *Critical Essays on Dostoevsky*, ed. R. F. Miller, Boston, Mass., 1986.

Nabokov, V., 'Fyodor Dostoevski'. In *Lectures in Russian Literature*, London, 1982.

Peace, R., *Dostoyevsky: An Examination of the Major Novels*, Cambridge, 1971.

Perlina, N., 'Herzen in *The Brothers Karamazov*', *Canadian-American Slavic Studies* 17 (1983), pp. 349–61.

Varieties of Poetic Utterance: Quotation in The Brothers Karamazov, Lanham, New York, 1985.

Reynus, L. M., *Dostoyevsky v Staroy Russe*, Leningrad, 1969.

Tri adresa F. M. Dostoyevskogo, Leningrad, 1985.

Rice, J. L., *Dostoevsky and the Healing Art: An Essay in Literary and Medical History*, Ann Arbor, Mich., 1985.

Sandoz, E., *Political Apocalypse: A Study of Dostoevsky's Grand Inquisitor*, Baton Rouge, 1971.

Solovyov, V. S., *Tri rechi v pamyat' Dostoyevskogo*, Moscow, 1884.

Steiner, G., *Tolstoy or Dostoevsky: An Essay in Contrast*, London, 1959.

Sutherland, S. R., *Atheism and the Rejection of God: Contemporary Philosophy and The Brothers Karamazov*, Oxford, 1977.

Terras, V., *A Karamazov Companion: Commentary on the Genesis, Language, and Style of Dostoevsky's Novel*, Madison, Wisconsin, 1981.

'Turgenev and the Devil in *The Brothers Karamazov*', *Canadian-American Slavic Studies* 6 (1972), pp. 265–71.

Thompson, Diane O., *The Brothers Karamazov and the Poetics of Memory*, Cambridge, 1991.

Todd, W. M., '*The Brothers Karamazov* and the poetics of serial publication', *Dostoevsky Studies* 7 (1986), pp. 87–97.

Van der Eng, J. and Meijer, J. M., *The Brothers Karamazov by F. M. Dostoevskij*, Paris and The Hague, 1971.

Vetlovskaya, V., *Poetika romana Brat'ya Karamazovy*, Leningrad, 1977.

Volgin, I. L., *Posledniy god Dostoyevskogo: Istoricheskiye zapiski*, Moscow, 1986.

Wasiolek, E., *Dostoevsky: The Major Fiction*, Cambridge, Mass., 1964.